Table of Contents

MW01484295

Dedication

This book is dedicated to Jennifer Lynn Milburn. Love engulfed and defined her very nature. In life, she taught us how to love, and in death, she taught us how to live. Her radiant smile was infectious and her laugh contagious. She was a role model of excellence and may her memory last a life time and her altruistic nature live on forever. My heaviest regret is that my children will never have had the opportunity to meet you and allow your glow to shine upon them. However, when they love, when they laugh, when they smile, I will share with them the story of their greatest cousin. You're a legend… So rest assured knowing, legends never die.

In Loving Memory

October 28, 1979- October 19, 2006

Acknowledgements

I would like to start by thanking you for choosing to read this book. For the past seven years, reading and listening to books, mostly non-fiction has become a passion of mine. I attempt to read and listen to everything I can get my hands and ears on, and I want to thank every author of every book I have ever read or listened to. If not for the culmination of different perspectives and insights offered by these authors, some very profound, I would have never ventured down the path of writing a book myself. I would like to specifically send my gratitude to Rupert Colley, an author of the *History in an Hour* Series, who gave me words of encouragement that inspired me to see this book through to the finish. After reading multiple books of his, I reached out to him on my quest to penmanship. His words of encouragement and the fact that he went out of his way to aid me, will not be forgotten. I highly recommend that you read his work… it is brilliantly fulfilling.

I would also like to thank my loving and doting wife Danielle, and my two beautiful daughters, Marlo and Berkley. You ladies are my moral compass and have granted me the "time of my life." To my Parents, who from a young age, instilled in me the importance of obtaining an education and provided me role models and heroes to emulate. To my in-laws, who from the very beginning accepted me as one of their own. You are grand and such an added joy in my life. To my extended family, you are tremendous examples of success and thank you for granting me the opportunity to have the most wonderful family a boy could grow up with. The experiences we have shared are reminders of what a family is all about.

I would also like to thank my former students, who encouraged me to publish this book and those who offered insights on how to improve it. You, along with some of my amazing colleagues, epitomize why I never work a day in my life. To my close friends, who spent the time to read and reflect their own insights on the development of this book. They are Sergio Meneses, Nick Webb, and Matt Ferrell. Without their thoughts and suggestions, I would not be as proud of this piece as I am.

I have been truly blessed with the most amazing people throughout my life.

I

Preface
Kids Will Be Kids:
A World War II Parable

While at a social event for my brother-in law's birth-day, I got to talking with a small audience around a fire. As we began speaking about subjects in high school that we had enjoyed or shown disdain for, one of my acquaintances piped in, "I hated history in school. History is all about boring facts and dates. Who cares about what happened years ago? The past is the past."

Now considering this isn't the first time I have heard this, and certainly not to be the last, I began by retort-ing William Faulkner, "The past is never dead. It's not even the past." As his facial expression contorted in an attempt to process the weight of Faulkner's quote, I rolled on, "Although you make some valid points, allow me to tell you a story that you know very well, that may change your perspective on history." He quickly agreed, and I vividly described the inspiration-al and world renowned Biblical tale involving *David vs.*

Goliath. As I moved through the story, I attempted to hold his attention by offering any tidbits that may have eluded him over the years. I walked him through the story, from the beginning to the end. From the moment the young Israelite David rebuffed the sword, helmet, and armor offered by King Saul, and instead, chose a weapon he had been more accustomed to, his slingshot. As he struck Goliath with the stone that hurled him to the ground, David took no chances, and quickly closed the distance between he and Goliath. As he towered over the disoriented giant, he unsheathed Goliath's sword and beheaded him right where he lie.

Instead of stopping there, I asked him if he could identify the parallels from the story that transcend into his own life. As he stood on in silence, I first proclaimed there was a powerful message behind David choosing his slingshot over the sword. And it was a message that is inspiring to each and every one of us. The lesson: young David didn't collapse under peer pressure from the Israelites, who urged him to grab a sword instead of the slingshot, or buckle because the Philistines were mocking and laughing at his underwhelming size. Instead, he chose to stick to his strengths, remain true to himself, and "do what he do." Secondly, the message that David conveyed to all of us around this fire, this very night, deals with David beheading Goliath and ultimately ending the giant's life. The message here is that whether speaking of a boss, a peer, an interview, or illness, there are no *giants* in life. We are all equals and nothing is too difficult to bear with the proper preparation and grit. To further illustrate, the lesson serves as a reminder to all of us… That when one places his faith in something larger than himself, prepares himself relentlessly to achieve greatness, and trusts the process of hard work and dedication, *anything* is not only possible, it is quite *attainable*.

While captivating their attention, I went on with another story, which too transcends time. The story was during a time when most traditional powers used slaves to do the tedious and small task of rowing their vessels across great distances. It is a story that involves a renowned sea-warring people who would use lightning attacks to devastate the coasts of Northern Europe. These men were so feared and revered, that each year, countries would make their own prayers, pleading God for protection and safety from these *Vikings*. However, each year and without warning, the Vikings would strike at random, and pillage entire towns and villages without mercy. In the hopes for survival, these villagers would barricade themselves behind thick woodened doors and shields. However, following a few precise strikes, these obstacles would crumble beneath them… and the Vikings would come for them. What separated the Vikings from most seamen and powers at the time wasn't their ruthlessness or cunning, but instead the fact that the Vikings rowed their own 20 ton vessels, over great distances.[i] As the legendary Pittsburgh Steelers football coach Chuck Noll quipped, "Champions are champions, not because they do anything extraordinary, but because they do the ordinary things better than anyone else." It was the Vikings who developed and harnessed incredible strength and power by rowing themselves, and choosing to repeatedly perform a seemingly small and tedious task.

The life lesson that transcends time and rows into our own lives, is that to find greatness, do the little things better than others. An example: One of the things I attempt to impress upon my students and players is that, if they wish to achieve their goals and dreams in life, they need to be better communicators. However, they must do the ordinary things, the *little* things, better than others. These little things could be as *seemingly* small as giving a firm handshake; or making eye contact; or possessing the ability to carry on a conversation with others; or showing up to work earlier than others; or giving a complement to the persons they come into contact with; or getting one's sleep so that they can display energy and enthusiasm throughout a day; or simply by offering a radiant smile. In short, to significantly impact your life and find success, identify and focus your attention on the attainable *little* things.

As the fire hissed next to us, I went on to say, that every event in history provides us with a learning opportunity, a lesson, or an inspiration that we can draw from and apply to our own lives. Whether around a fire or sitting in history class, these stories provide meaning to our lives. We can use these stories to improve our lot in life, and to pursue the happiness that Thomas Jefferson had envisioned for us. For that is what history is full of… Anecdotes of triumphs and failures, of individuals, who thrust in the midst of adversity, displayed the courage or cowardice, grit or defeatism, simple luck or lack thereof, to place *their* name within a chapter of the coveted book called *History*. Now, I cannot say that those two stories changed his negative perception of history, or healed any wounds inflicted from past history teachers, but I can say that he found more appreciation of it.

As a history educator and lifelong learner, I have read lengthy books and truly enjoy the facts and information they offer, but what I have found imperative is transforming those facts into stories to better engage my students into the content. I firmly believe that with teaching history, less is often more. I have always attempted to "sell" to my students the concepts and lessons provided by history, rather than over-indulge them with the content of it. In short, it is not my goal for students to memorize facts and regurgitate them on a test, but to challenge them to think *historically*. That is not to say that the content lacks importance, because it is essential. It is the content of both of these stories, David and Goliath and the Vikings, which allow us to bring it to life. However, it is the concepts of those stories that transcend time. When people challenge themselves to think *historically*, they can use history as a moral compass and inspiration. For history becomes a bore for students and pushes them away when all you offer are the dull facts on a PowerPoint. People want to hear stories and long for relevance in their lives. One way to instill a love of history is to place a figurative mirror in front of students and make it relatable to their own lives, their own choices. If we can do that, I whole-heartedly believe that we can change some of the negative misconceptions about history being nothing more than a rolodex of facts and dates. History, if approached conceptually and not just factually, can be interesting and valuable to everyone. People should use history to travel beyond descriptive story-telling, and into something more prescriptive and applicable to gain appreciation, understanding, and inspiration for our own lives. One does not have to venture long or far into history to realize the success stories within its annals.

There have been countless individuals, both renowned and anonymous, who have turned their hardships into a success, not an excuse.

History offers much more than what many persons give it credit for. The cause-and-effect relationships in history, the decisions of a country's leader, the choices of a country's population, and the responses to those choices, offer insightful and inspiring lessons for us to live our lives with purpose and meaning. For instance, World War II is a beacon of light for finding such purpose and meaning. For instance, the Battle of Britain provides lessons of solidarity and resolve. The Battle of Stalingrad is about downright resiliency and the determination to overcome all odds. The Holocaust shows the dangers and the sheer horror of what discriminating and bullying others can lead to. The attack on Pearl Harbor provides a conflicting lesson between meticulous preparations versus the lack thereof. These lessons are applicable to one's own life, whether in regards to a profession, to an interview, within sports, or even parenting. Its' range is truly endless. To further illustrate, Pearl Harbor presents a lesson of the perils stemming from a persons' failure to learn from the past. To quote James Bradley, author of *Flyboys*:

The unsuspecting navy ships lay peaceably in their Pacific harbor that winter morning. A world away, the drowsy sailors' commander in chief had been negotiating with Japanese diplomats. But then, with no advance warning, Japan launched the infamous sneak attack. Deadly torpedoes and bombs came out of nowhere, and soon the harbor was a flaming mess of sunken ships. Screaming sailors swam for their lives through fiery oil blackened waters.

President Roosevelt admired the sneak attack. "I was thoroughly well pleased with the Japanese victory, the president wrote his son."

Maybe Teddy would have felt differently if the sailors had been Americans. But it was the Russians who were taken by surprise that morning at Port Arthur on February 8, 1904.[ii]

If this was a true account of Japan's actions just a few decades earlier, how could America's leaders, military brass, and its' people become so surprised on December 7, 1941? One should be no more surprised when a snake acts as a snake or a drunk behaves like a drunk. To maximize history's full potential, one must possess the expertise and willingness to learn from the past. As a country that morning, we learned a valuable lesson about the perils that come from the collective failure to draw from the past. Historical events can both inspire people to pull through life's challenges, and break them away from simplicity, by daring their minds to climb to greater heights.

To find the connections between the past and the present, one must remain curious. Curiosity is the most powerful motivator to development and learning. It is curiosity that draws a child to a hot stove, a television, a toy, or anything for that matter. This book offers a parable or an analogy and comparison to World War II. This parable will elicit curiosity and challenge readers to delve more into the motivations, decisions, events, and ramifications of a complex subject. This is a parable that offers simplicity, yet, challenges one to explore the unknown, answer questions, and find growth in the process of learning.

Although history is full of seemingly unrelated events and people, they are in actuality as intertwined as Henry Ford is to the automobile. For every action there is an equal and opposite reaction. Furthermore, for every inaction, there too are consequences. History is considerably riveting when analyzed and viewed through Robert Frost's poem, "The Road Not Taken," or Ray Bradbury's short story, "The Sound of Thunder." These are masterpieces that can be used to explain history and incite a reader to ask the "*what-ifs*." Mr. Frost's poem and Mr. Bradbury's short story can be interpreted that for every seemingly *small* action, there can be a *great* consequence. On the flipside, the poem and short story can be also be construed, that for every inaction, there too are consequences. Considering this book is a parable about World War II, one must look deeper into the characters' actions and inactions to grasp the powerful connotations to history. All in all, I challenge you to play the role of a favorite fictional detective, research events in history, and view each historical event with the same thoroughness as a crime scene. Put on your proverbial rubber gloves, comb for prints, and uncover the motive behind each action…in short, remain curious.

Considering historical events are similar to crime scenes, they should be viewed with the same intensity and focus. Therefore, they should be handled by the best gumshoes, their detective kits, and their cunning ability to follow a hunch to the guilty party. If viewed in the same light as a crime, the end of World War II would become known as the most destructive, horrific, and wretched crime scene in history. One could argue that even the Grim Reaper became saddened and fatigued from cleaning up the horrors of World War II. An estimated 60 to 80 million people met their premature deaths during that struggle. To be more precise, roughly 45-million of these dead were not soldiers equipped with the newest guns of the time or pilots strapped in the cockpits of the latest planes… but women, children, and the elderly who simply tried to survive their hellish realities.

Does it take a considerable amount of time to explain all that transpired during World War II? Amazingly, the answer to that question has been a resounding no. As time goes on, subtleties of events turn into digestive realities. American history has oversimplified World War II to consist of a little more than an attack on Pearl Harbor, a Holocaust, a mad man, and an atomic bomb. For American history, this oversimplification dates back to the founding of the United States of America. For example, the decisive Battle of Saratoga, which brought the French into the Revolutionary War, was actually won by Horatio Gates, not George Washington. However, most Americans would respond by saying, "Horatio who?" Considering that history, generally speaking, has been oversimplified to feed the small appetite sought after by the average mind, the answers to events are found with relative ease. To pacify this psychological phenomenon, people created the website Wikipedia. An unintended consequence of Wikipedia in regards to researching major historical events has been the crippling of minds to an extent where persons are unwilling to scratch deeper than the surface. This parable's goal is to provide a well-balanced culmination of both oversimplification and complexity through a descriptive writing style. It is not my intent to overindulge the reader with historical facts or overanalyze each action, battle, or event in World War II. For the majority of readers, doing so would be on similar scale of over feeding the surviving "dissidents" of World War II who were discovered in the concentration camps spread out across Eastern Europe. When these "dissidents" were fed by Allied troops, many succumbed to an unsettling feeling of sickness, fatigue, or even death. It is not my intent to offend anyone, but with limited time and a limited willingness to expend energy on one topic, I want this book to be brief, yet captivating. In short, I hope to provide the reader with a short but insightful way to grasp World War II. This book's purpose is to incite and inspire one to research and dig deeper into the major events of World War II.

Upon reading and becoming inspired by the works of Spencer Johnson and his profound parables that rise above race, gender, profession, time, and age, I chose to write a parable covering World War II. If George Orwell could create a masterpiece by making pigs of men, I figured even the feeblest of minds could make boys of countries. Often times less is more; whether in terms of orated speeches, presentations, books, or conversations. Did you know that Abraham Lincoln's Gettysburg Address was only 273 words long? Or that Martin Luther King Jr's, "I have a Dream" speech, was roughly sixteen minutes in length? Although lengthy, detailed books are of necessity for experts and those aspiring to be, the average person will simply neglect a 650-page book concerning World War II, or tune-out a speaker who rambles on for hours. Instead, with a society that places a premium on time, people want to receive information in a concise, insightful, and efficient manner. Hence, I attempted to achieve just that in this short story. By seeing World War II through the actions of school children within a schoolhouse, this book provides a parable/story that offers a fresh, unique, and profound way to look at the greatest catastrophe of the 20th century. This book attempts to shy away from the dull and dreary, the minute details and the content associated with history, and veer away from how information is traditionally presented. Instead, this is a book that focuses on the concepts of each major event before, during, and immediately concluding World War II. The concepts are based off of the content, just in a simplified form.

First and foremost, the message of the book is reinforced by the title *Kids Will Be Kids: A World War II Parable*. It refers to the old adage that basically explains kids do what they do because that's what they've always done. In other words, in the rudimentary sense, history repeats itself. Each character found within the pages of this book represents the involved nations and their actions during the melodrama of World War II. Each of these actions and their roles, subsequently, led to its start in September of 1939 and its eventual conclusion in August of 1945.

World War II and the Holocaust are two of the most documented events in all of history. They have both been researched with proper diligence and the respect they deserve. World War II incites so many people to study it because it offers unlimited interests to its readers and researchers. The war contains stories, concepts, and profound lessons about heroes and villains, both the horrors and beauties of war, weaponry and tactics, blunders and brilliance, bravery and fear, deception and truth, persecution and love, romance and betrayal. Furthermore, it is a war filled with science, organization, leadership, sociology, and much more. Lastly, World War II makes up the world we live in today. Hadn't Europe entangled itself into two horrific wars (both World Wars) within two decades, America would not stand as the sole superpower today. I will expound on this further later in the book. As a result, for all of the reasons listed, I chose to write a book concerning World War II because I too have always been infatuated with it.

Even though a reader would have to delve into additional books to fully comprehend World War II, the transgressions within this book could be used to serve multiple purposes and to reach a variety of fronts. There are main derivatives that this book offers to a reader— it is refreshing and profound, it is simplistic yet challenging, and it is efficient and engaging. This book hopes to hook a reader into World War II by inciting the reader to ask questions and encourage him or her to investigate deeper into the dark but fascinating time period. The book's hope is that it inspires a reader to travel down the sometimes ambiguous path to that horrific event, by offering an innovative look at World War II.

To further illustrate,

This book offers a simple but profound way to view the events of World War II. If the reader has become a historian who has mastered his craft the way Sherlock did his and lifted the proverbial rock or retraced the steps that led to the conflict, this would be a good book to test one's knowledge on the topic. Many of the character's actions are subtle, and as a result, these subtle actions will test the intuitiveness of the reader. It challenges a historian to make the connections between the character's actions and the main events leading up to, during, and just following World War II. That being said, I included a "less is more" timeline at the beginning of the story, so that you may familiarize yourself with the major events before getting into the parable.

Lastly, as a history educator, the book offers a parable, where colleagues in the profession can use a different approach with their students to introduce or conclude World War II. As we all know, stories provide powerful avenues to relay information; they create memorable and lasting impressions, stir emotions, and construct strong connections between a character and an event. I am passionate and have become convinced that every student who reads this short story, with a teacher's presence and guided questions in hand, will draw the necessary connections to the past. It would be my greatest joy to have you enjoy this book immensely.

II

Sequence of Events

1914-1918: The Great War

World War I commenced with England, France, and Russia (Allies) waging war on Germany, Austria-Hungary, and the Ottoman Empire (Central Powers), primarily in Europe. Both sides fictitiously believed that due to the immense size of their militaries, new scientific technologies, and strong nationalist fervor, the war would be over within months. Instead, for those very reasons, the war became a monotonous stalemate. After both sides failed to outflank one another, which became known as the 'Race to the Sea,' both sides burrowed themselves into the earth with a military strategy known as trench warfare. The trenches became known as the Western Front and were primarily located in France throughout the duration of the war. The German army displayed its military prowess as it successfully waged a two-front war, between Britain and France in the West, and Russia in the East. Eventually, due to heavy losses, starvation, and a disconnected Czar Nicholas II, Russia broke out in Revolution in 1917, overthrew their Czar, and capitulated from the war. As Russia bowed out of the war, Germany was able to focus their entire attention in the direction of France and England. As a result, in the final year of the war, Britain and France were on the ropes and the German army had neared Paris. However, to the relief of the Allies, at the end of 1917, America joined the war and saved the day. While fresh, America used their might to push the Germans back, and force an armistice in November, 1918.[iii] Some historians argue that while Germany celebrated their country's fallen during the Great War, the French, English, and Americans attempted to move on and forget about the war and those who were senselessly sacrificed.[iv]

1919: Treaty of Versailles

The Treaty of Versailles officially ended World War I, but it will unfortunately lead to a greater war. It was extremely harsh on Germany: As was evident with 414 of the total 440 provisions punishing Germany.[v] Five of the provisions made Germany take full responsibility for starting the war, give up overseas territories, cede their land to Poland, Belgium, France, and Czechoslovakia, fork out large war reparations, and decrease the size of their army and navy to nothing more than a national guard.[vi] By the early 1930's, unemployment reached a staggering 25% in Germany, and many Germans believed that their economic hardships stemmed from the harsh conditions under the treaty. Hitler and the Nazi party used this German resentment towards the treaty as a launching pad to gain power. If in power, the Nazis promised to rectify past injustices and nullify the treaty. As a result, historians view this as the major antagonist and catalyst to the Nazi party and Adolph Hitler coming to power within Germany. This took the world down a path of a Second World War, subsequently, altering the name of the Great War, to World War I.

1927: Chinese Civil War

China broke out into a civil war between Chiang Kai-Shek's Nationalist forces and Mao's Communist forces.[vii] An already inferior Chinese military now became fractured, which allowed Japan to occupy parts of China.

1929: Stock Market Crashes

Throughout the 1920's, Germany needed money from America to pay France for war reparations; France needed money from Germany to pay their war debts to England; and England needed money from France to pay their war debts to America.[viii] This vicious cycle came to a devastating halt when the Stock Market crashed and the world fell into economic peril; due largely to a lack of world-wide trade. As a result, some democratic governments collapsed and militaristic dictatorships took root.

1930: Maginot Line

As Germany could no longer afford to pay reparations to France, another war between Germany and France seemed inevitable, and the French began to construct the magnificent defensive structure, the Maginot Line.[ix] Drawing on the style of fighting used in World War I, the French believed that the best offense in war was a great defense. The Maginot Line consumed most of France's military spending and cost roughly $7 billion in total. Furthermore, it crippled the French into a defensive mindset and lulled them into a false sense of security… For they believed that as long as they stayed behind the defensive fortifications, they could repel any German attacks. As a result, this defensive mindset hindered them from creating an offensive strategy in dealing with Germany. This allowed Germany to pick the time and place for the fight with France in the future.[x] In short, the French failed to identify that mechanized technological enhancements in tanks and airplanes had drastically altered military tactics since World War I. Due to this development, within a decade, the French would pay gravely for this mistake.

1931: Japan invades Manchuria

While China was preoccupied in a civil war, Japan invaded the northern region of China called Manchuria. Japan needed more resources and living space for their growing empire, and they found much of it in this region. The League of Nations condemned the attack, but without a fighting force, it showed the world that it would do nothing to stop the Japanese, or anyone else for that matter. The resounding message was that the League of Nations was weak and it was not to be respected. This will foreshadow the League's unwillingness and inability to curb future actions.

1933: Hitler in Power

If you were a German in 1933, you were more than likely a member of one of two political parties; the Nazi Party or the Communist Party. The majority of Germans joined the Nazi party, and voted in President Paul von Hindenburg installed Adolph Hitler as the Chancellor of Germany. Within a month of Hitler's appointment as Chancellor, the German Parliament headquarters, the Reichstag, burnt to the ground and by September 1934, he became Dictator/Fuhrer of Germany. By the end of the year, 100,000 German Communists and opponents were arrested, tortured, or murdered in concentration camps.[xi] As a totalitarian-style of government took root, with Nazi informants seemingly everywhere, parents had to be careful of what they said to their children, phone calls were monitored, and everyone realized quickly, that it was no longer safe to speak out against the Nazi party. As individual freedoms were revoked, fear gripped the German people.

1933-1938: Persecution of the Jews

Soon after Adolph Hitler stepped into office in 1933, persecution towards the Jews began. To further illustrate, Jewish children were segregated from German schools and others were removed from public professions; such as doctors, lawyers, and professors. In 1935, things worsened for the Jews when Adolph Hitler enacted the Nuremberg Laws, which stripped Jews of German citizenship and banned marriages and intimate relations between Jews and non-Jews. As a result, thousands of persons of Jewish descent began to see the writing on the wall, and sought avenues of escape from Germany. Furthermore, Nazi officials encouraged people of Jewish descent to migrate out of Germany. However, to leave, Jews were required to leave behind 2/3 of their financial wealth, their house and its' belongings, and anything else that they could not carry.[xii] Those most fortunate, escaped to America or England. Other Jews were able to escape to countries surrounding Germany, but little could they know that these countries would soon be occupied and under the Nazi German yoke. Another roadblock for Jews was the fact that many countries either began setting immigration quotas on Jews, or barred them completely from immigrating into their country. As a result, the unfortunate stayed behind, and held onto the hope that things would not worsen. From November 9-10 of 1938, a year before the start of World War II, the persecution turned violent in Austria and Germany, known as Kristallnacht, or the "Night of Broken Glass." During the two-day orgy of violence, 1,200 synagogues were damaged or burnt to the ground, thousands of Jewish shops and businesses were vandalized and their property was stolen, and 30,000 Jews were sent to concentration camps. Bewilderingly, Jewish owners had to pay to repair any damages to their shops.[xiii] If there was any doubt before, the remaining Jews in Germany now knew that they had to get out of the country. However, now it had become too late.

1935: Italy invades Ethiopia

Italy, under Fascist dictator Benito Mussolini, invaded Ethiopia for its resources. Again, the League of Nations stood by and did nothing.

1937: Japan invades China

In a quest to garner more resources, Japan attacked deeper into China and waged a full scale war on the divided nation. Japan's military carried out a policy known as the three "All's": Kill all, loot all, and burn all.[xiv] Nanking, the capital of the Nationalist government, became home to one of the darkest chapters of human cruelty in the history of civilization. Within the city, Japanese soldiers raped, murdered, and tortured Chinese civilians, both male and female, old and young alike. Estimates claimed that up to 200,000 Chinese women, from the ages of 8-80, were raped by Japanese soldiers.[xv] With this brutality and the negative press circulating around it, the American people began to turn on the country of Japan.

1936-1938: Appeasement & Munich Conference

Between these years, Hitler refused to abide by the Treaty of Versailles by militarizing the Rhineland, annexing Austria, and taking control of the Sudetenland in Czechoslovakia. Hoping to avoid another war at all costs, France and Great Britain stood by and did nothing; reinforcing the notion of appeasement in their dealings with Germany.[xvi] Appeasement gave Hitler the time, confidence, and resources needed to build a military machine that would become unrivaled in Europe. Neville Chamberlain, Prime Minister of the United Kingdom, sat down with Hitler in Munich, Germany, and informed him that he could have Austria and the Sudetenland, but he could take no more. Hitler agreed to the demands. As Chamberlain returned to Great Britain, he falsely proclaimed to the world, that he had secured "peace for our time."[xvii] This false assurance only reinforced to the English and French people that they could avoid war with the serpent. Hitler soon made Chamberlain look the fool.

1939: World War II Commences- Poland invaded

Hitler rightfully gambled that if he sent the majority of his military forces into Poland, France and Britain who were not yet ready for war, would stand idly by and do nothing. However, Hitler knew Germany was not yet prepared for war with the Soviet Union, and consequently signed a non-aggression pact with the Soviet Union, promising to split Poland with their eastern neighbor. With assurances of non-aggression, Hitler sent the German military into Poland. As a result, Britain and France declared war on Germany, and World War II commenced. However, Britain and France were not yet prepared for war and refused to intervene militarily in Poland.[xviii] Thus, Poland became a sacrificial lamb for the upcoming onslaught. As the

Poles were fighting valiantly for their survival in the west, against a mightier German army, Russia invaded Poland from the east, and Poland was forced quickly to capitulate. American leaders stood by, helplessly watching the world's events unfold for the worse. With America's involvement in a European war (World War I) still too fresh on their citizens' minds, American leaders knew that its' people were wrapped too tightly in an isolationist mindset, and would not want to become enticed into entering another European war.

1940: Trade embargo on Japan

Both the brutal actions committed by Japanese soldiers on Chinese civilians, and the fact that Japan's growing empire was infringing on America's Pacific empire, American leaders placed a trade embargo of oil, gasoline, and scrap metal on Japan.[xix] As Japan saw a war looming with America, Japan began preparations of carrying out a devastating and crippling attack on America at Pearl Harbor.

1940: Fall of France

Following the collapse of Poland, from September to April, a "Phony War" ensued between England and France with Germany. Both sides were making their final preparations for war. Neither the French nor the British knew that Hitler was only waiting for the weather to clear to launch a German attack. As spring came and brought more suitable weather for Germany's Panzer tanks and mobilized units, Germany feinted a heavy attack (Manstein Plan) into northern Belgium and Holland. Hitler's military advisors had hoped to draw British and French forces from their defensive posture in France. Aiding Hitler's ploy, French leaders had promised their citizens that unlike World War I, this war would not be fought upon their soil. As a result, the Allied forces of Britain and France quickly took the bait and marched unknowingly into the trap in Belgium. As Allied military leaders remained skeptical about the German Luftwaffe allowing their forces to march into Belgium unimpeded, Germany sent their main force through southern Belgium and the Ardennes Forest, which cut off the British and French's supply lines. While British and French forces became hemmed up onto coastlands of northern France, they realized their hopeless plight. All the while, the Germans drove a remarkable 40 miles per day into the heart of France. However, as bad as things were, the British saved themselves from complete defeat through the largest military sea evacuation of its kind in history from the port city of Dunkirk. However, due to the poor French leadership, a lack of reserves to launch a counter offensive against the initial German breakthrough, and a lack of will to enthrall themselves into another war, to the world's astonishment, France quickly fell within six weeks to the Germans.[xx] As Hitler returned from France, he received "cheers to the heavens" from his German people. Hitler had achieved more in nine months, than any German ruler in history had accomplished in a lifetime.[xxi]

1940: The Battle of Britain

With the fall of France, the British now faced the German war machine alone. Some in the British parliament had hoped to seek peace through the Italian dictator, Benito Mussolini, and Hitler offered it. However, Winston Churchill, Britain's newly elected Prime Minister, dismissed the notion. Churchill argued that there had been no real fight as of yet, and stated, "Nations which went down fighting rose again. Those which surrendered tamely were finished."[xxii] As the British refused to surrender without a fight, the "Battle of Britain" would rage on for the next eighty days. In preparation for German soldiers to invade the island of Great Britain (Operation Sea Lion), Hitler's had hoped to use the dreaded German Luftwaffe to first control the skies over the island. However, the combination of Britain's radar, the capability of the British to use radio communication from the ground to their pilots, and the lack of a clear or consistent plan by German command, led to disastrous results for the German Luftwaffe. As frustration set in, Hitler ordered the commencement of the "Blitz" on London, where German bomber and fighter pilots rained bombs and terror on London. All in all, there were 90,000 casualties from the Blitz. However, instead of weakening the morale of the British, it increased their willingness to fight.[xxiii] Furthermore, as the German Luftwaffe suffered heavy losses, Hitler was forced to abandon an invasion plan of the British island. Instead, he now focused his gaze towards the Soviet Union.[xxiv] During this same year, the Tripartite Pact was signed between Germany, Japan, and Italy. These countries became known as the Axis Powers.

1941: Operation Barbarossa

Two major events transpired in 1941 that changed the course of the war and eventually led to the defeat of the Axis. The first was Operation Barbarossa. Hitler long desired Russia's vast resources and land to help fuel his German war machine and supply his people with immense land and wealth. As a result, Germany used recently acquired western Poland to launch, up until that time in history, the largest military invasion in history with a surprise attack on Russia. On the same day as Napoleon's invasion of Russia in 1812, nearly three million German soldiers spilled across the border, and within the first week, drove 200 miles into Russia.[xxv] Overwhelmed and overmatched Russian soldiers were forced to retreat, while millions of Slavs, Communists, and Jews were rounded up by a merciless unit called the Einsatzgruppen, taken to the outskirts of towns and shot and buried in shallow graves. This brutality eventually backfired on the Germans, as the Russians understood that to surrender to the Germans, was to die. Due to the deep penetration of the German military, Russian factories in the west had to be completely uprooted and relocated deep within the Ural Mountains. Some world leaders believed that it would only be a matter of weeks before Russia surrendered.[xxvi]

1941-45- Holocaust & Final Solution:

Nazi leadership viewed those who were Gypsy, Jewish, homosexual, and mentally or physically handicapped, as subhuman and dissidents of the German state. More perplexing, as the Nazi rule extended east and controlled a large tract of the Soviet Union, they could not figure out what to do with the large Slavic population. As a result, under the orders and implementation of Hitler, Heinrich Himmler, Adolph Eichmann, and other the Nazi leaders carried out a ruthless and systematic campaign to entirely eradicate these persons from Europe. Depending on ones' age, handicap, or gender, many of these 'dissidents' were sent directly to the gas chambers; many others were sent to work camps where they were fed meager rations that led to starvation, disease, and death; many were simply rounded up and executed outside of towns and villages; and some were even used in inhumane scientific experiments. In 1942, the Final Solution, the pogrom to eliminate all of these "dissidents," was enacted by a senior Nazi official, Reinhard Heydrich. However, the shorthanded Nazis will receive help from collaborators within other countries to locate these targeted groups of people. For example, officials in France, Romania, Italy, Czechoslovakia, etc., will help the Nazis round up and transport these unfortunate groups of people to the killing fields and concentration camps throughout Europe. Through this collective effort, by the end of World War II, four out of five Jews in German occupied Europe died as a result of the Holocaust.[xxvii]

1941: Pearl Harbor

Americans, while in an economic recession and still gripped tightly to the idea of isolationism, were still in no mood to involve themselves into another European war. However, following months of preparation, Japan carried out a surprise attack on the United

States at their Pacific Naval base in Pearl Harbor. The sneak attack was a great short-term success for Japan and became the worst military disaster in American history. Without a Pacific fleet, America became entrenched in a very vulnerable position and had to quickly rebuild its' lost navy. The next day, America declared war on Japan, and in turn, due to the Tripartite Pact, Germany and Italy felt compelled to declare war on America.[xxviii] However, the Tripartite Pact only bound Germany to come to the aid of Japan, if Japan were attacked. Nevertheless, under the false presumption that Japan could fully occupy America's attention, and that Germany was invincible, Hitler made the mistake of declaring war on America. As a result, Hitler's hubris gave American leaders the excuse they had been looking for to fight the German aggressors. Furthermore, the attack did not lead America to sue for peace, as Japan had hoped, but instead, the dubious attack inspired the nation to break out of its' isolationist mindset and provided America with the resolve needed to defeat the Axis.[xxix] The entry of the United States into World War II provided some much needed support to both Great Britain and the battered Soviet Union.[xxx]

1942: Battle of Midway

Midway served as America's most westward military base, and Japan had hoped to seize the island and create a greater buffer from itself and America. Instead, this would serve as the greatest naval achievement in American history. As America broke the Japanese military code, they knew when, where, and how the Japanese would carry out their next attack. As a result, America led Japan into a trap at their Midway atoll military base and waited to spring the trap. As the Japanese fighter planes took flight from four Japanese aircraft carriers and attacked the American base, most of their ammunition and fuel was spent. Furthermore, while the remaining Japanese planes rested on the decks of the four aircraft carriers, they had been fitted with torpedoes and bombs, and served as highly volatile explosives.[xxxi] As a result, when the American dive bombers swooped in, three of the Japanese aircraft carriers were sunk within minutes, and the fourth only moments later. While suffering minimal losses, America won the Battle of Midway, and took the upper hand in the war in the Pacific Theater. This allowed America to choose the time and place for every battle here on out with Japan. Furthermore, America used an island hopping strategy, where they jumped from one island to another, until they slowly tightened the noose around the island of Japan.

1943: Germany's Catastrophe in Russia

As the winter set in and the German advance slowed to a halt within Russia, the German Sixth Army, with limited winter clothing, no anti-freeze, a lack of proper supply lines to feed their troops, and a very strong adversary, became ill-equipped to endure the cold Russian winter and became bogged down inside of the Russian city of Stalingrad. As a result, the entire German Sixth Army, while freezing and starving to death in Stalingrad, became completely surrounded by the Russian army and was forced to surrender. By the end of the year, all could tell that the tide had now turned in the Russians favor and Germany eventually faced catastrophic defeat.[xxxii] In hindsight, it was the defeat at the battle of Stalingrad that altered the war from a potential German victory, to a guaranteed defeat.

1943-1945: Italy surrenders and liberation

In the hopes of creating a feeling of hopelessness and despair with the German people, and to draw the Germans away from the coast of Normandy, the Allies planned to knock Italy from the war. After they first conquered Sicily, and then fought into mainland Italy, the Allies fought a brutal campaign against the German soldiers stationed within Italy. As Italian citizens never fully supported the war effort, when things took a turn for the worse, King Victor Emmanuel III had Fascist dictator Benito Mussolini arrested and Italy switched to the Allied side. However, too weak, the Italians were unable to rid themselves of the German presence. Furthermore, as German soldiers and Hitler felt betrayed, German soldiers stationed in Italy, began burning and looting.[xxxiii] However, the Germans refused to leave without a ferocious fight, and it would cost the Allies 312,000 casualties in total, in the 608-day struggle to liberate Italy.[xxxiv] As Anglo-American forces landed on the shores of Italy, they fought slowly and painstakingly up the Italian boot, to push the entrenched Germans out. On June 4th, 1944, two days before the landings at Normandy, the Allies captured Rome. All the while, the Allies received an enthused welcome from the Italian population. It would not be until May 1st, 1945, that Italy was fully liberated by the Allies.

1944: D-Day

Through the use of decoys, spies, and repeated army broadcasts, the Allies feign an attack at Pas de Calais. However, the real attack will be on the beaches of Normandy. The deception pays off, as the Germans take the bait and focus much of their military might at Pas de Calais, giving the Allied assault an advantageous chance of succeeding.[xxxv] When D-Day commenced, 150,000 Allied forces landed on five separate beaches in Normandy, France. After some intense fighting, the Allies succeed in securing the beaches and establishing a beachhead. Although unexpected hedgerows in northern France slow the Allied advance, they will punch through and eventually liberate France. This will place Germany between an Anglo-American assault from the West and a mounting Soviet offensive in the East. Seeing that it was futile to continue the war, some German commanders attempted to assassinate Hitler.[xxxvi] The assassination attempt failed and the war waged on.

1944: Operation Bagration:

Purposely launched on the third anniversary of Operation Barbarossa, the Soviets began their long and arduous march towards Germany to enter the beast's lair. Although the invasion became overshadowed by D-Day, this was one of the largest military campaigns throughout the entire war. With the punishing and painful memories of the German invasion of Barbarossa still fresh on their minds, the Soviet soldiers marched towards Germany with the callousness and ruthlessness of an Asiatic horde. "The hour of revenge has struck," and "smash, burn, and have your revenge," were echoed by Soviet leaders and propagandists. Consequently, Soviet soldiers will murder, plunder, and rape with reckless abandon on their trek

towards the heart of Berlin. As reports of these be-
haviors surfaced, the Eastern German people became
stricken with panic and fear. As a result, many Eastern
Germans gathered what they could and dashed west
towards the advancing Americans.

1944: Battle of the Bulge
The Battle of the Bulge was the last major effort by
the German forces to push the Anglo-Americans out
of France and back across the English Channel. After
initial success, the Anglo-Americans were thrust
backward (creating a bulge in the Allied lines). However, the Germans ran out of fuel and were overwhelmed by the superior strength and numbers of the
Anglo-American forces, and were crushed.

1945: Battle of Berlin
As the battle for Germany's capital commenced, most
able-bodied German soldiers had been killed or had
surrendered. This left the city primarily defended by
the elderly and the very young. On April 30, while the
fighting waged in the streets between Russian soldiers
and German civilians, Hitler married his girlfriend
Eva Braun, before both of them committed suicide.
On May 8th, as it lay completely in ruins, and with its'
ruthless dictator dead, Germany officially surrendered.

However, for the next ten years, Russian soldiers raped up to three million Eastern German women. Consequently, the hell for Berliners and East Germans was far from over.[xxxvii]

1945: Atomic Bombings

Following the intense fighting between American and Japanese forces for the Solomon Islands, Guadalcanal, Guam, Iwo Jima, Okinawa, and others, and the very few Japanese soldiers willing to surrender, American leaders realized an invasion of mainland Japan could exceed one million casualties. With American support waning at home, and a lack of sufficient funds to carry on the war for an extended period of time, America looked to another option. The Manhattan Project, initiated in 1942 by Franklin Roosevelt, was the secret military project that led to the creation of an Atomic bomb in 1945. Following Franklin Roosevelt's death in April, 1945, new President Harry Truman was informed about the power of atomic energy, and how it could potentially end the war. Truman was left with a difficult decision to make: fight for years and spill more American blood, or use the atomic bombs to put an end to the war quickly. Truman lets his decision be known at the Potsdam Declaration in May, 1945, as he gave Japan the ultimatum to surrender unconditionally or face "utter destruction." However, Japan refused to surrender unconditionally, and held out hope that they could receive a favorable peace negotiation. That hope was extinguished with the introduction of the atomic bomb. Two American bombers, on August 6th and August 9th, dropped an atomic bomb on the cities of Hiroshima and Nagasaki, respectively. Upon seeing the devastation of the atomic bombs, on September 2, 1945, Japan officially surrendered to America and World War II came to a close.[xxxviii]

1945-1991: Cold War

In 1945, the Cold War began between the United States and the Soviet Union. With contrasting economic and political philosophies, neither side agreed on what a post-war Europe should look like.[xxxix] Holding onto the belief that World War II could have been avoided, America pushed for an industrious and economic prosperous Germany. The Americans argued that Hitler came to power because of the harshness of the Treaty of Versailles, and that a strong and independent German economy would prevent future unrest. On the other hand, following two German invasions in the Soviet Union over the past twenty years, subsequently killing over 30 million Soviets, the Soviet Union pushed for an agricultural and economically weakened Germany.[xl]

Due to the fact that both sides were unwilling to come to an agreement, Germany was divided into two countries, East Germany and West Germany, and Berlin was split into two cities. As a result, over the next forty years, the city of Berlin became home to a blockade, a tank standoff, and the Berlin Wall. Furthermore, it is the place where the two sides, America and the Soviet Union, waged their differing economic and political philosophies. While America promoted Capitalism and Democracy, Russia campaigned for Communism and Totalitarianism. The end would not come for forty plus years, as the Soviet Union collapsed unexpectedly from within.

III

Map & Illustration

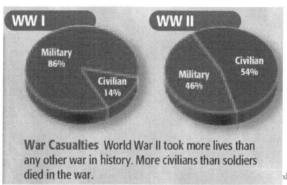

War Casualties World War II took more lives than any other war in history. More civilians than soldiers died in the war.

xli

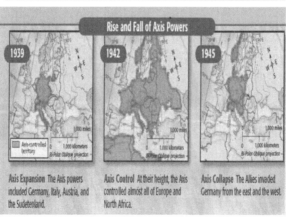

Axis Expansion The Axis powers included Germany, Italy, Austria, and the Sudetenland.

Axis Control At their height, the Axis controlled almost all of Europe and North Africa.

Axis Collapse The Allies invaded Germany from the east and the west.

xlii

IV

Poppa's Story

"Incoming fire. Get down! I said get down! Machine gun and tank fire are tearing through our infantry lines. The Germans are overrunning our positions. I say again, we need support now," Charlie orders commands to his troops.

Charlie knows his men are brave and that they are the best trained soldiers in the world. On top of that, he is convinced that he's as inspiring as Martin Luther King Jr., that he possesses a military mind as great as General Robert E. Lee, and that he is as skilled a fighter as a Navy SEAL. He is reassured that these men, if asked, will fight to the last breath for him.

"I thought these Germans were finished, done for. But they attack us again?" Charlie mutters to himself incredulously.

Charlie, while covered in camouflage and strapped snugly in his black army boots, has masterfully concealed his body to the ground. His plan is to jump up, charge straight ahead into the teeth of the enemy, and drive them back on their heels. His mind has become flooded with promises of honor, glory, and courage, and he intends to seize them all.

He grasps his machine gun tightly and orders his men, "On the count of three, I want these Germans retreating backwards and crying for their mamas. One. Two. Three. Charge!"

His performance would not disappoint. His machine gun raises with lightning speed, and his aim is impeccable. He moves with the agility of an assassin and lays down one German next to another. As he continues his surge forward, he pulls a grenade from his pocket and launches it at an advancing German tank. Boom! The tank is quickly forced out of action. Simultaneously, he levels his machine gun again and fires a burst into a crowd of incoming Germans. One by one, they fall lifeless to the ground. As he bobs and weaves through the battlefield, a bullet bites into his flesh. No time to stop moving forward, no time to bleed. He pushes forward on adrenaline and guns down the perpetrator. His act of defiance sends fear into the German lines, and they begin to buckle under his constant approach. As they begin to fall back in hopes of survival a voice calls out.

"Charlie! Charlie!" Charlie's father hollers. "It's time to go to Poppa's house."

The mentioning of Poppa snaps Charlie back to reality and away from his reenactment of the Battle of the Bulge. He surmises that, thanks to Poppa, the Germans will live to see another day. As Charlie drops his toy machine gun, he sprints toward his father in elation of going off to see his grandfather. The excitement of it all is too much to bottle up. He has been waiting for this day since his ninth birthday, when Poppa had promised him that, next year, he would read to him the "Kids Will Be Kids" story of all stories. It was a story that Poppa had promised would overshadow all of the other stories he had read him up to that point. So, like a countdown to Christmas, Charlie had begun to mark his calendar thirty days out from his tenth birthday. He knew turning double digits was a momentous event, and the beloved toy machine gun his father had gotten him was evidence of that. But he knew that even it wouldn't compete with Poppa's "Kids Will Be Kids" story of all stories.

As Charlie eagerly threw himself into the passenger seat of his father's pickup truck, his memories flashed back to all of the stories that Poppa had shared with him over the years. These stories were filled with such imagery and such vivid detail that he was able to fully immerse himself into them. Also, Poppa had a way of simplifying stories that allowed young Charlie to understand them. And Charlie knew, as a World War II veteran, Poppa had some really exciting experiences to share.

As his father turned onto the long and winding driveway leading up to Poppa's house, Charlie could barely contain himself. The home, an old farm house, stood with a sense of purpose, a sense of pride. The house was a fitting salute to someone from America's most revered generation. As the truck rolled to a stop, Charlie's feet hit the ground and speedily climbed the four steps leading up to the towering door. Just as Charlie reached for the doorknob and readied himself to impatiently barge into Poppa's house, the door swung open, and Poppa's arms swallowed up his young grandson. With a tight but loving squeeze, Poppa raised Charlie's feet off of the ground and brought his beaming face to his. An Oscar performance could not match the level of love and adulation the two stared at one another with.

Poppa: "Happy birthday Charlie. I have missed you. You're getting so big. You're going to be tall and strong like your dad in no time."

Charlie: "Poppa, I have been marking my calendar for this day since last month. I am so excited to hear your "Kids Will Be Kids" story of all stories. I told all my friends at school about it and told them not to worry, for I would tell them all about it next weekend at my birthday party."

Poppa: "Charlie, the story will have to wait until after supper. Now run in there and get washed up for dinner. I cooked your favorite meal — meat loaf, peas, and corn on the cob."

Charlie: "Okay, Poppa. Thank you."

After Charlie's grandpa and father conversed and embraced one another, Father drove off, and Poppa readied supper. As Poppa served Charlie a plate and set it in front of him, he could see that the food would not suffice him for long. Normally, Charlie would have taken his time and savored every bite. But this wasn't a normal night. This was the night of the

"Kids Will Be Kids" story of all stories. And he wanted to get to it as soon as Poppa was willing to tell it. Heck, Charlie would have skipped dinner if Poppa had allowed him to. As Charlie shoveled down the last of his peas, he sprang out of his chair and bolted for Poppa's rocking chair. The time had come, and Poppa knew his ten year-old grandson could no longer wait patiently. Poppa would have liked to hear more about Charlie and what he was learning in school. However, he accepted his fate, cleaned off the table, and met the boy in the den. As he walked into the room and saw Charlie, he was reminded just how much he relished reading stories to Charlie. He realized that he had adored reading stories to Charlie just as much as the youngster enjoyed hearing them. Even though healthy at this instance, the death of far too many loved ones over the years had helped him appreciate these precious moments with Charlie. Charlie's intuitiveness, passion, and enthusiasm toward his Poppa had helped forge a special bond between the two. They truly needed one another, and it was never more obvious than during story time.

Before taking a seat in the rocking chair, Poppa reached up and grabbed the book that Charlie had so excitedly desired over the years. Ever since its introduction, Charlie wanted to read it, and hadn't it been locked, would have done so by now. And locked it was indeed. Countless times over the years, Charlie had crept down Poppa's staircase and got his hands on the book. To his chagrin, picks, hairpins, random keys from his grandpa's house, and hangers could not break open the lock's mighty grip. Charlie had become convinced that the book's lock was protected by some form of magic, and only Poppa could break its spell. Out of fear of Poppa finding out about his mischievous late-night dealings, he always returned the book back to the exact spot he had found it. In actuality, unbeknownst to Charlie, his attempts to open the book had been a running joke for quite some time between Charlie's father and Poppa. Just about every time Charlie stayed the night at Poppa's, the lock had mysteriously gained additional scratches to its surface. With the book in hand, Poppa sat down on the rocking chair, and Charlie plopped down on his lap. "Well, Charlie, are you ready?" Poppa asked.

"You bet I am, Poppa. I wouldn't miss this for the world," Charlie responded.

As Poppa's fingers dug into his breast pocket, he retrieved a small golden key, and handed it over to Charlie.

"Do you want to open it?" Poppa teasingly prodded.

"Oh, Poppa. Really?" Charlie hungrily questioned.

"Anything for my Charlie —," Poppa replied with a radiant smile.

Charlie guessed this was what pirates felt like just before opening a treasure chest. As the key slid into the slot, Charlie turned it until he heard a click and opened it. Charlie examined the book for a moment, until Poppa tenderly grabbed it from his hands. It took Poppa no time to begin reading aloud. "'Kids Will Be Kids: A World War II Parable.' By Poppa …"

V

Prologue

A Shadowy Figure Looms
Worldwide Depression: A Dilapidated Schoolhouse
World War I: Commemorating the Past

If life and history can be simplified down to the core of Robert Frost's poem, "The Road Not Taken," and is a consequence of a choice between one of two paths, then we certainly chose the wrong one.

As the wind bounced off of the chimes, they listened intently and could hear it sing sad songs for the dark future that lie ahead. Millions worked tirelessly through fatigue and sweat by day and night. To them, the noise was deafening and surreal. However, to the human ears, not a creature was stirring. As they indiscriminately chomped relentlessly, piece by piece, they were not seen nor heard. They had all done this before and knew that they were right on schedule. Unbeknownst and unannounced to the human dwellers on the floor above, as their left feet stepped in front of their right, and vice- versa, was that this building had been infested, and all too soon, the walls would crumble around them. Leaders would point fingers and plead in hindsight that those small and quiet creaking noises should have been addressed long ago. However, as a car in the bottom of a lake represents "too late," so too does this particular story of termites and its metaphoric connection to the failure of the Treaty of Versailles and the League of Nations. The culmination of each small bite eventually led to the greatest, most inhumane conflict to date — World War II.

The temperature dropped noticeably, leaves began to stir restlessly from the incoming wind, and the swings, which had been resting peacefully in place, began to sway into the air as if they were embracing the grip of toddlers. A storm was brewing, and it was in hot pursuit of the shadowy figure who traveled at a brisk pace to his destination. Although the figure had been accustomed to the violence of the human race since Cain and Abel, he was in disbelief that they could be so reckless and unwise in such short time. The upcoming trouble had triggered his keen senses long ago, but he still had delayed his departure from his comfortable abode... for he was certain that due to his last visit and the millions left dead in his wake, cooler heads would prevail. Little did he know at this particular moment that that calculation would serve to be an empty dose of optimism. As he approached the site, his memories hummed like an irate hornets' nest. The recollections of the roughly eleven million boys that he had tirelessly carried on into the afterlife exhausted him to no end. He believed it had been a task that would not come to bear again for at least another millennium, only after it had been completely forgotten and time healed its deep inflictions. The figure would soon be proved wrong, and for that, he would become extremely disappointed. As he hovered to a halt atop his journey's endpoint and glided gently down into the fenced-in schoolyard, everything looked eerily similar to his arrival twenty-one years before.

As the figure's eyes lifted from the schoolyard and rested on the schoolhouse, he first noticed the abundance of flags waving and flapping from its rooftop. Each flag was hung proudly by a particular boy, who claimed his as his own. These flags highlighted the differences between the occupants in the schoolhouse, and in due time, its walls would prove to be too small for its diverse inhabitants. The enormous size of the structure was something that was truly astonishing. To illustrate its grandiose size, the Empire State Building and the Eiffel Tower were both dwarfed and swallowed up by its presence. However, for its magnificence in size, in terms of appearance, there was little to be desired. The figure felt that since his last visit, the enormous structure had aged significantly. Leading up to the door, he was immensely underwhelmed by the battered siding, the outdated window panes, the decrepit staircase — which lacked any luster or appeal — and the railing, which was originally designed to keep kids from falling off a five-foot drop-off, now looked as stable and safe as a small boy resting upon the saddle of a wild horse. Moreover, as the chimney sat upon the aged and waning structure, it spewed out a thick, black smoke into the air that gridlocked the would-be beautiful, bluish sky hovering above. To a keen observer, the chimney foreshadowed the darkness that was to come.

Along the tree line of the schoolhouse, laid two unkempt monuments that stood side by side; both monuments were dated 1914- 1918, and while one was written in French and the other in English, they were etched with three somber words, "The Great War." Abandonment would be the word the figure would use to sum up the sight around these two pillars. Grass surrounding them held one another up as a trainer does a boxer who has seen far too many rounds; the hedges, whose sole purpose was to provide a serene backdrop, instead provided only a cluttered setting that stole the onlooker's gaze from the monument itself; and the tree limbs hung over and cast dark shadows, drowning out the bright summer sun beneath them. Both monuments reeked of desertion and were reminiscent of an ominous past that prayed hard to be forgotten.

On the other hand, there stood a monument about forty yards to the east that was written in German. As beauty is to ugly, the German monument would serve as an excellent example of an antonym to its French and English neighbors. It permeated a sense of honor and remembrance for its fallen during "The Great War." Surrounding the German structure, grass had been manicured to the extent that it looked surreal; the hedges were neatly clipped into a sharp and defined edge that only a person who had mastered his profession would have been able to muster; while the trees provided an almost poetic backdrop to the monument itself. The figure concluded that the graceful scene would have aroused even the most uninspired artists to go and fetch their easels, canvases, and brushes. This German monument exhibited an appreciation and gratefulness for its country's fallen.[xliii]

Just as he considered exploring further into his surroundings, from inside the schoolhouse, a woman's voice could be faintly heard through the increasingly prevalent gusts of wind. As the figure looked skyward, he knew that the storm that had been stalking him since he had begun his trek had eluded him no longer. The sun cowered behind the clouds, and a shadow swept over the area like a monsoon. Considering that the inhabitants had awakened the storm a second time within a twenty-one-year period, the figure knew that it was seeking retribution. As the figure cautiously approached the schoolhouse, gingerly climbed the rickety steps, and peered through the window, he was exasperated. It did not take long for the Angel of War to realize that he had backbreaking work ahead of him, and that this schoolhouse and its schoolyard would once again be doused with death, carnage, and destruction.

VI

Calm before the Storm

Cast of Characters

Li'l Adolph —Germany

Li'l Austria — Austria

Li'l Benito —Italy

Li'l Chiang —Nationalist China

Li'l Czech —Czechoslovakia

Li'l Eliezer —Jews

Li'l Ethiopia —Ethiopia

Li'l Franklin —United States

Mrs. League —League of Nations

Li'l Mao —Communist China

Li'l Paris —France

Li'l' Polanski —Poland

Li'l Stalin —Russia

Li'l Tojo —Japan

Li'l Winston —England

"World War I, also coined the Great War, was such an atrocious scene. While artillery and machine gun fire ripped holes through the night, boys at the average age of nineteen bunkered down in trenches, in the hopes of surviving another day. These boys lived in constant fear of being chased down and butchered by the same fate that left millions of others their age dead. This war was on a scale and magnitude ..." Mrs. League paused for effect and eyed each of the children as they looked on, enamored with her story. "On a magnitude that would change the landscape of warfare forever. It reached levels of carnage, destruction, and despair that have yet been matched in history. Nations throughout Europe armed millions of boys with machine guns, flamethrowers, rifles, poison gas, and grenades, pitted them against each other, and senselessly sacrificed them in the name of nationalism, imperialism, and militarism. These boys were cruelly hurled into "No-Man's- Land," and were swallowed up by the barbed wire and enemy fire that awaited them. All the while, as the machine guns finally silenced and the last artillery shell fell, most of these nations hoped to convince their citizens to disremember the war and its trivial beginnings. Never in history have millions of boys been more deceived and betrayed in the name of pride and honor than in World

War I. This is why, I repeat, we have to learn from the mistakes of the past. We cannot- ever- put people through the pain and suffering that gripped this world twenty-one years ago. As a piece of clay can be formed into a fine piece of art, the past forms the present and can help to predict the future. We should be able to prevent anything like this war I speak of, of happening ever again." As Mrs. League preached her "sermon" to the on looking students, tears filled her eyes, along with the eyes of many of the boys in the classroom. This was a reminder that these boys were intimately close with many of the men, who, as boys, had fought in that conflict and relayed down many of the stories from that horrid time and vile war. These boys heard from the mouths of those who had fought in that war and their proclamations of the massacres and bloodshed that came with it… the war to end all wars. Most of the eyes that were fixated on Mrs. League knew that they never wanted to be personally responsible for repeating this catastrophe that engulfed nations throughout the world. Mrs. League, as she stared intently at a red-faced and angered little boy who wore a brown uniform, went on voicing her own prejudices and interpretations of the Great War to the class, "And Germany started World War I and had to be punished for all of the destruction and suffering. She had to be brought to her knees and was so as a result of the Treaty of Versailles. Rightfully, the once-proud Germany had to pay war reparations, shrink her military to a minute size, and lose both acquired land overseas and the land surrounding it." As Mrs. League stated this, a few of the students nodded their heads in agreement.

Like a scalpel into tissue, Mrs. League's words cut sharply into Li'l Adolph's psyche. At Mrs. League's mere mentioning of World War I, he began stewing and brooding with anger and malice in his heart. Just as Mrs. League finished lecturing, Adolph rose with his neatly pressed brown uniform with a Nazi swastika attached to its sleeve, and passionately shrieked, "It wasn't Germany that lost that war! What lost that war were the Jews, the Communists, and the traitors of Germany who forsook their fatherland to the treacherous Allies." As he spoke fervently, his veins protruded out from the sides of his neck and forehead like an animal stretching the leash that restrained it. "Germany will enact revenge. And that revenge will come very soon," Adolph vowed.

The surrounding classmates consisted of Li'l Paris, Li'l Winston, Li'l Franklin, Li'l Tojo, Li'l Stalin, Li'l Chiang, Li'l Benito, Li'l Polanski, Li'l Eliezer, and a few smaller boys. As Adolph theatrically spoke, his hands waved methodically, and with the exception of Tojo and Benito, the classmates sat on, saturated in disbelief, horror, and shock at his choice of words. Adolph, who only five years ago was a scrawny weakling compared to his fellow classmates, had built himself up to be the most strapping and intimidating presence in the one-room structure. He had become the classroom's leading bully and had instilled a fear, a respect, or both from every one of his fellow classmates. Just recently, in defiance of Mrs. League's guidelines, Adolph refused to pay his school fees, stole school supplies, food, and money from some of his fellow classmates, and surpassed his authorized physical strength requirements. For example, he was required by Mrs. League to not possess weapons or bulk his physical prowess. However, while ignoring such restrictions, his wallet became stuffed with cash, his resources were plentiful, and his bulging muscles caused his shirt to stretch exhaustively to the brink of tearing. However, either out of fear or apathy, no one dared to challenge him. Consequently, as a result of this appeasement from Mrs. League and the fellow classmates, Adolph took more and more from his peers. For example, Li'l Austria and Li'l Czech were placed under the German yoke and forced to dress in gray Nazi uniforms, sport the swastika with pride on their sleeves, and be horrifically cruel to one particular student. Additionally, they gave Adolph complete control over their every movement and action within the confines of the schoolhouse. Inconceivably, none of Adolph's peers, or Mrs. League herself dared to challenge him … at least, not just yet.

The particular student that Adolph eyed with contempt was the much smaller Eliezer. As Adolph grew in power, any good fortunes that Eliezer had previously obtained melted away like snow in a thaw. To make matters worse, every classmate turned a blind eye to the constant and malicious treatment of Adolph toward him. Through restrictions Adolph himself coined the "Nuremberg Laws," Eliezer was repeatedly reminded by some of his classmates that he was beneath them and that he should disappear or be eradicated from their sight. Also, Eliezer was forced by Adolph to wear the Star of David on his sleeve to signify that he was Jewish and to methodically brand him as an outcast. This left him at the cruel mercy of some of his anti-Semitic peers. Out of fear of provoking an attack, Eliezer sat on as mute as an iceberg to the constant harassment. However, unbeknownst to Eliezer at the time, this would not be the extent of his misery, only a precursor of what was yet to come.

Mrs. League, a frail and fragile woman, had earned
very little respect from her students over the years and
was unsuccessful in her attempts to get them to follow her classroom guidelines. Her lack of control was
a two-part problem: First, neither Li'l Stalin nor Li'l
Franklin would support her; and secondly, she was
not allowed to carry a paddle to instill discipline. The
lack of respect became obvious four years earlier
when Li'l Benito, right in front of Mrs. League and
without protest, began taking things from a smaller
and weaker peer named Li'l Ethiopia. Then again two
years later, the lack of respect toward Mrs. League re-
surfaced with her inability to control Li'l Tojo, as he
began bullying and harassing the enormous but flabby
and distracted Chiang openly and defiantly. Tojo, with
a militaristic mind-set reminiscent of Adolph and with
limited resources himself, took full advantage of his
superior physical strength to steal Chiang's resources.
It didn't help Chiang's cause as he became deeply distracted and committed to fighting another boy, Mao.
Now, as a result of the most recent turmoil with
Adolph, Mrs. League fell apart and faded into oblivi-
on. Never to be seen again.

In light of these events, the students became masters
of their own dominion, and every decision shaped the
fate of the schoolhouses' future. However, it was the
inaction of the past that would soon doom all of their

fates. The thought of instigating another war on the magnitude of their predecessors had overrun most of them with fear. As a result, the class had allowed Adolph to become too mighty to control or intimidate.

The Angel of War cast his gaze to many of the young boys around the room. He quickly noticed a sizable presence covered from head to toe in the colors red, white, and blue. It was Li'l Franklin, a boy who he had recognized as the kid who years earlier, saved Li'l Winston and Li'l Paris from a certain and embarrassing defeat at the hands of Adolph. Although the size of Franklin impressed the Angel of War, it was the recollections of Franklin's bravery, intensity, and might that resonated most. However, at the present moment, Franklin sat, hunched in his chair, and looked completely disinterested in his surroundings. Franklin had grown to regret immersing himself in the last fight between Winston, Paris, and Adolph. As a result, he had made a stern commitment to distance and isolate himself from any future conflict.

Next, the figure's eyes fluttered in disbelief to the cruelty that Tojo bestowed upon Chiang. Tojo, while flashing a wicked smile, repeatedly and ruthlessly beat

Chiang over the head and prodded him. The inhumanity that Tojo carried himself with was unsettling and turned the stomachs of all on lookers. Although lacking in size, Tojo made up for it in ferocity and intensity. Over the years, Tojo sat on, defenseless, as he watched the "white devils" — Winston, Paris, Franklin, and some of the other boys —bully weaker classmates in the name of religion. Out of fear of falling prey to these white devils and in the hopes of attaining equal power and wealth, Tojo began equipping himself with the most modern technology, enhancing muscle to his small frame, and bullying those he considered weak.

The figure then noticed Paris and Winston huddled up and talking quietly in the corner. As his ears tuned in, the figure overheard them agree to confront Adolph with an ultimatum. After the brief meeting and while depicting a strong facade, Winston and Paris gathered the courage to sit Adolph down and tell him that he could keep what he had already taken, but if he took one more thing from anyone in the room, a vicious war would ensue. Winston and Paris held onto the illusion of hope that war could be averted, so they did not yet prepare themselves for it. They had both reasoned to themselves that Adolph should be fully sufficed, for he had taken back everything that had been stripped from him years ago. They simply

couldn't fully fathom that Adolph would want more.
However, if they had had the ability to foresee the
near future, they would have been appalled to find out
what was yet to come.

VII

Might of the Axis

A Soviet and German Pact: An Uncommon Bond
World War II Commences
Fall of Paris: An Unforgiveable Defeat
Battle of Britain: Story of Resolve
Operation Barbarossa: Loyalty of a Serpent
Pearl Harbor: Japanese Deception

The Angel of War looked on with the understanding that arduous work lay ahead. As a result, an undefined sadness fell about him like the dark cloud anchored overhead: For he had seen all of this violence transpire before, just over twenty years earlier, and he knew the ominous suffering that came as a result. He unsuccessfully searched for answers to elusive questions: How could this all happen again so soon? Didn't he provide enough carnage, death, and obliteration last time? What could he have done differently to eradicate any inclination for these people to do this again? His inquiries were snapped short by the deafening thunder that tore a hole through the sky. The sound sent animals scattering in all directions in search of shelter from the upcoming storm. The Angel of War knew the time had come. He looked on with malice in his heart, and his lips muttered to themselves that if this is what they wanted, this is what they would receive in full. He ensured that compared to last time the devastation would be six-fold. He vowed that this time, they would learn the hard lessons of inhumanity. No rock would be left unturned.

Like spotlights, the classmates' eyes scoured the room. They nervously waited on the edges of their seats for any inkling of aggression. Polanski, although terrified, prepared himself for the upcoming onslaught that was certain to come from Adolph, who for quite some time had been eyeing his resources. At the same time, while standing across the room from one another, Franklin and Tojo glared at each other in a deep-rooted distrust that dated from events in years past.

Instead of being grateful for his recent acquisitions, Adolph surreptitiously passed word to Stalin to forge an unlikely alliance. Adolph, a strong anti-Communist, told the Communist-minded Stalin that if he agreed to keep the peace between the two, he was willing to share Polanski's resources. Stalin, whose sported attire was exclusively red, held a hammer in one hand and a sickle in the other. Although very strong and by far the largest presence in the class-room, compared to Adolph, Stalin was still the weaker of the two. For it was only two decades ago, that Adolph had crushed Stalin mercilessly, and forced him to cry out in defeat. In addition, Stalin surmised that if he could make a friend from a foe, he could focus on other more pressing needs. For these rea-sons, Stalin excitedly approved the secret agreement. At that moment, unbeknownst to Polanski, his fate had just been cast, stamped, and sealed.

On September 1, 1939, while all of the boys stood outside in the schoolyard, harmony dissipated quickly. Peace vanished like the luminous warmth from the sun when it cowers behind an endless cloud. While ignoring the pleas from classmates and with a set of demonic eyes out in front, Adolph stalked Polanski. In a fair fight, the average-sized Polanski would be a formidable opponent to most boys in the classroom. Unfortunately, for Polanski, this did not include Adolph. Therefore, as a lion realizes that it is within reach of its dinner, Adolph sprang and closed the gap quickly with the smaller-sized Polanksi. Yet, to Adolph's surprise, the peer stood staunchly in opposi-tion and had decided that he would not to go to his grave without protest. Instead of crumbling in fear,

Polanski fought with a tenacity that would have made a Spartan who had fought at the Battle of Thermopylae proud. He absorbed Adolph's best punches and delivered defensive parries of his own. For this reason, like fireworks bursting into the night, classmates saw flickers of hope and resolve flash brightly in his eyes. Some actually began to reason that it was possible for Polanski to fend off the bully and his lightning attack. However, as quickly as the underdog story grew in stature, it faded away. In spite of his valiant effort, the treacherous actions of a boy standing to his rear proved insurmountable. With Polanski's full focus and energy directed at Adolph, Stalin rose up from behind Polanski and, with a thunderous might, landed a collection of unopposed volleys with his hammer to the back of Polanski's defenseless skull. Stalin's blows came down unopposed and became as fatal as the fang of the world's most venomous snake. As a result, just as quickly as his eyes had flickered with hope and resolve, they now dimmed with bleakness and despair. As Polanski's consciousness waned under the constant barrage, he cried out in desperation for Paris and Winston to intervene. However, Polanski's cries fell on deaf ears, and his situation became as hopeless as a butterfly net catching the wind. With a silence as deep as death, death became his fate.

The oppressive German and Russian yokes were set upon Polanski.

The Angel of War's eyes locked onto his first victim and his sharp, razor-like talons followed with the swiftness and the precision that would have made first-class snipers insecure with their marksmanship. Polanski lay lifeless on the cold floor, his soul representing the millions of spirits that now filled the Angel of War's cage-like contraption, which hung loosely down his side on the end of a metallic chain. The metallic chain looked as if it had been weathered from its constant use over the centuries.

As both boys finally understood that Adolph possessed further ambitions for continued conquest, Paris and Winston reluctantly declared war on Adolph. Before the pronouncement of war, both Paris and Winston were mentally in a state of appeasement, and physically, they were softened by the hopes of a long-lasting peace. Nevertheless, due to the sudden shift toward war, they hurriedly began sharpening their weapons, honing their skills, and building up the strength and courage to stand toe to toe with the class bully. As their eyes fell about the imposing figure towering over Polanski, who lay broken at his feet, they held on to the hope that as long as they stood side by side, they would come out of this war victorious.

Adolph, who carried away only a few minor cuts and bruises from the fray — and with a pact with Stalin that left him no threat to his rear — turned away from what was left of Polanski and set his full gaze in the direction of Paris and Winston. The two could see the hatred that consumed him — a hatred that they both knew had been ignited and fueled by a perception of an unjust past. While kicking up dust, Adolph's feet marched methodically and forcefully toward the two proven fighters, Paris and Winston.

Paris, who was equal in size and a kid who had become renowned for his fighting prowess, readied his hands in preparation. Memories flooded into his mind of the two prior conflicts he had had with Adolph in the schoolyard, each boy coming out a victor in one of the two fights. It was well documented that both kids loathed and distrusted one another.

Winston, on the other hand, was smaller than the other two in both height and weight but carried with him the heart of a lion. Winston, through the use of a cunning mind, a zealousness to deliver a bloody lip, and a pair of quick hands that would sting an opponent into submission, had manhandled his classmates over the years. Consequently, Winston had built a reputation for himself that was unmatched by anyone in the schoolyard.

As the gap between Adolph and the others closed, a brief scuffle ensued between Adolph and four pint-sized boys who were unfortunately standing in his path. After taming them with relative ease, Adolph instructed the four runts to slip into the gray Nazi uniforms and join Austria and Czech in bullying Eliezer. Afterward, Adolph walked up and stood face to face with Paris and Winston, their noses a cat's whisker away from one another, nostrils flaring like heat from a furnace, and hands clenched at the ready. The showdown between the three had finally arrived, and the tension in the air could be cut with a wooden spoon.

Paris stood tall with supreme poise in his defensive prowess. Upon learning the best maneuvers against Adolph during the Great War, which brought Paris victory, his confidence in his defensive strategy was well- grounded. Soon to be to his demise, Paris stubbornly held on to the notion that the best offense was a strong defense. Incredulously, Paris had forgotten that his latest victory over Adolph was less to do with his own physical competence, and more to do with Franklin's heroic acts. Paris' fabricated belief in his defenses led to an over-assurance of his strength. On the other hand, Adolph, drawing from his past short-comings with Paris, had practiced and mastered the techniques to break through such readied defenses. And with relative ease, a breakthrough is what he would attain.

Considering Adolph detested Paris and seeing that he stood nearer out of his two opponents, his goal was to knock Paris from the fight swiftly and convincingly. Adolph hoped to hit Paris so hard that it expelled any fight from Winston. Adolph, the rage unleashing itself like a bat into the night, threw his first punch, which traveled at lightning speed around Paris's defenses and landed squarely on his chin. The velocity, trajectory, and brutality of that first punch extinguished much of the fight in Paris, and his eyes became flushed with fear and panic. The second blow, which seemed to come at a bullet's pace after the first, landed on the side of Winston's head, also sending him sprawling backward in a stupor. As Winston sat on helplessly in a haze, he looked on in bewilderment at what transpired next.

Benito, who stood nearby, watched Adolph pummel
Paris and send Winston into a partially dreamy state.
One couldn't help but notice Benito budding with a
renewed confidence, due to the strength of his new
found friend Adolph. As a result, like a poker player
betting confidently on a winning royal flush, Benito
jumped into the fray and aided Adolph in finishing off
Paris. As Paris' arms hung limply at his sides, another
punch arrived and speedily swelled his eye. Like a
priest exorcising a demon, the punch extinguished any
last tenaciousness from the already deflated opponent.
Adolph stood over the pathetically wretched boy, and
readied himself to rain down the blow that would hurl
the Angel of War to Paris' side. However, rather than
proving himself resilient, and finding a way through
his plight, Paris surrendered as the sun does to a pass-
ing cloud and collapsed in the face of adversity. By
and large, a fly caught in a spider's web would have
exhibited more fight in it than the renowned Paris.
Shortly thereafter, Paris sheepishly fell under the
German yoke, climbed into the gray Nazi uniform,
wore the swastika, and, as Adolph instructed, began
bullying Eliezer. Although Paris may have escaped
with his life that day, he knew that he had left his reputation to the vultures on that schoolyard for years to
come.

The fellow classmates watched in astonishment to how hastily Paris succumbed to defeat and how seemingly powerful Adolph was. Even Adolph was astounded by the relative ease of it all. As Winston's senses came back in full, he rose to his feet and tried to grasp the dire situation he now saw himself in. Paris, his strongest ally only moments ago, now wore a matching swastika to Adolph. Stalin was a potential ally, but he was sharing the bed and its covers with Adolph. Lastly, there was the robust but currently unfit Franklin, who had come to his aid the last time he and Paris fought with Adolph and who had single-handedly pulled them from the jaws of defeat. He wondered if he could be so fortunate again. Winston knew that Franklin was gripped tightly in an isolationist mind-set, and he didn't want to get involved in another fight that did not directly affect him. Still, Winston held out optimistically that, in due time, Franklin would join the fray and would once again herd him from the slaughter. However, until that day arrived, Winston knew he would have to hold out against all odds and will his way through this.

With Paris muzzled like a dog, Adolph's entire focus now became fixated on the small but scrappy Winston. Before he went in for the kill, with compassion

in his voice, he asked Winston, "Why don't you capitulate? It will save you from the severe and embarrassing beating that I gave Paris."

Winston, although filled with anxiety and doubt from
his current predicament, unexpectedly became swept
up by a wave of courage. This enabled him to deliver
an inspirational speech that would be remembered for
centuries to come. With a face tempered like steel, he
stoically scoffed at Adolph's surrender offering with,
"Even though a large tract of Europe and many old
and famous States have fallen or may fall into the grip
of the Gestapo and all the odious apparatus of Nazi
rule. We shall not flag nor fail. We shall go on to the
end. We shall fight in France and on the seas and
oceans; we shall fight with growing confidence and
growing strength in the air. We shall defend our island
whatever the cost may be; we shall fight on beaches,
landing grounds, in fields, in streets and on the hills.
We shall never surrender and even if, which I do not
for the moment believe, this island or a large part of it
were subjugated and starving, then our empire beyond
the seas, armed and guarded by the British Fleet, will
carry on the struggle until in God's good time the
New World with all its power and might, sets forth to
the liberation and rescue of the Old.[xliv]

Like a great orchestra hitting its climax, Winston's voice was filled with a feverish pitch as he continued, "The battle of France is over. I expect the Battle of Britain is about to begin. Upon this battle depends the survival of Christian civilization. Upon it depends our own British life, and the long continuity of our institutions and our Empire. The whole fury and might of the enemy must very soon be turned on us. Hitler knows that he will have to break us in this island or lose the war. If we can stand up to him all Europe may be free, and the life of the world may move forward into broad, sunlit uplands. But if we fail, then the whole world, including the United States, including all we have known and cared for, will sink into the abyss of a new Dark Age, made more sinister, and perhaps more protracted by the lights of perverted science. Let us therefore brace ourselves to our duties, and so bear ourselves that, if the British Empire and its Commonwealth last for a thousand years, men will still say, "This was their finest hour."[xlv]

Like a lit match igniting a candle, these speeches provided a lift in morale and eradicated any doubt from within. Although Winston knew that it would be arduous to find his way through this, he vowed to cower thoughts of defeat each and every time it offered itself.

Unmoved by Winston's pronouncement, Adolph began raining down a score of punches atop of Winston's head. As a result of the barrage, blood began to trickle from Winston's scalp and down his forehead, and swelling shortly ensued. Although the punches came at a frequent pace and found their way through Winston's defenses, there he still stood in growing defiance. To Winston's advantage, metaphorically speaking, his back was against the wall, and at no time is a person more desperate, more intense, and more dangerous. Every punch Adolph sent was answered and replied two-fold by Winston. The fight was reminiscent of a meeting between two glorified fighters, who while in their prime, attacked one another with the desperation and stubbornness to hold on to the lore of their legacies. As the fight waged on, it became obvious that Winston would not shrink, but instead, grow in stature. The fortitude that Winston displayed stole any hopes from Adolph that surrender loomed just over the horizon. Consequently, as a rider pulls the reins on a horse that approaches a cliff, Adolph slowed his punches and sent his focus eastward, in the direction of a peer who possessed a false sense of security. This hubris would eventually prove to be Adolph's downfall.

Because of his previous agreement of peace with Adolph and the seemingly good fortunes that accompanied it, Stalin beamed with a smile that radiated a supreme confidence. Thereupon, he stood lackadaisically and carried himself gleefully, with a carefree attitude, all the while, echoing a belief in a very bright future. However, as a dehydrated and dying man in the desert fictitiously sees an abundance of water, this confidence would prove to be a facade or an illusion. As Stalin was lost in his premature elation and premonitions of bliss, a sharp and intense pain screamed into his back, drowning out all of his senses. A pain jolted through Stalin's body with the magnitude and might of a powerful earthquake, and he painfully realized breaking bread with this serpent would lead him to the brink of surrender. Adolph smiled more and more intently as his knife, until recently concealed, penetrated down to the bone over and over again; striking Stalin down. As if enjoying the process with every grimace, Adolph used the sharp edge of the knife to breach Stalin's abundant frame. Stalin labored over in pain from the blows and was in despair from the betrayal of trust demonstrated by this monster disguised in human flesh. Opaque flashes began to engulf Stalin as he became more and more broken from the malicious strikes.

While the blows rained down on Stalin, Franklin attentively watched the carnage. He became a tad anxious about the events unfolding before him. Questions began flooding his mind: Would Adolph come next for him? Should he get involved in this fight to help Winston before it was too late? Would Stalin or Winston be able to recover from the early setbacks in the fight? As he looked on at the schoolyard, which now was a bloody mess, he was horrified at the level of ease and hatred with which Adolph carried himself with. Could anyone stop this menacing figure? If so, who? As Franklin searched for the answers to these questions, and as he hoped to find a way to involve himself whole-heartedly into the fight, a furious one-two punch tore into the side of his head. Franklin labored over in pain, his entire left side hanging lifeless.

His meticulous preparation into these strikes was time-consuming and could not have been delivered more skillfully and precisely to its intended target. Tojo had waited patiently for the perfect moment to attack Franklin — a time when it would be least expected. Tojo seized the moment when it arrived, and although the one-two punch supplied by Tojo was methodical and connected in sublime placement on the side of Franklin's face, it didn't have the impact that Tojo had hoped. Actually, it had quite the opposite effect. It was a one-two punch from Tojo that would have had most boys in the schoolyard suing for peace. However, this was no ordinary boy. This was the boy who only years earlier, had donned the cape and the letter S across his chest, as he rescued Winston and Paris from Adolph's tightening grip of defeat. Like a giant being awakened from a deep slumber by an unexpected pounding on the door, Franklin gathered his senses, stood with rage, and gained the whole-hearted motivation to push them through the challenging days ahead.

The intense fighting between the boys on the schoolyard was interrupted for a moment, as Franklin, with a mixture of grief, anger, and hatred, launched a thunderous scream. As the blood gushed from the side of Franklin's head, he sought out retribution, and like an enraged tiger, he carried a look in his eyes that sent shivers down the spines of onlookers. It cast a brief silence over the crowd. Almost instantaneously following the one-two punch, like dispensing air into a balloon, Franklin's muscles began to swell, and he grew in both stature and determination. Although Tojo vowed to remain relentless, he now knew that his days were numbered. All the while, Winston smiled, for he knew the time had come for Franklin to don that cape again and rescue him from certain defeat.

VIII

The Holocaust

A Tragic Tale

Eliezer, once a proud and confident boy, walked dejectedly in fear and shame. Over the last number of years, Adolph's treatment toward Eliezer had progressively worsened. The systematic and merciless reproach that he coldly served Eliezer had disastrous consequences. Adolph incorporated a four-step model to isolate, attack, and destroy Eliezer:

> First Action: He identified Eliezer as being different and inferior in comparison to every other boy in the class. He did this by berating him publicly and placing the Star of David on his school uniform. As the years passed, Eliezer noticed more and more of his peers distancing themselves from him.

> Second Action: Adolph further isolated Eliezer from his classmates when he stripped away his resources and money.

This weakened him financially and the tattered clothes and lack of material needs made him an outcast to the others.

Third Action: Adolph designated Eliezer to a specific area in the school house and forced him to stand there, all day and night. Out of fear, the poor kid shakily stood, withering away.

Fourth Action: Lastly, with the help of the other boys, Adolph began to physically assault Eliezer, punching and kicking him ruthlessly. This attack was on a scale that had never been seen before in all of the years the schoolhouse stood.

Following these years of constant verbal lashings and physical assaults, both Eliezer's mind and body began to deteriorate. His mind, as was evident in his demeanor, buckled under the unceasing pressure. This was evident when he no longer conversed with the other boys in the class, no longer bore any minute resemblance of a smile, and as he repeatedly questioned the existence of a God who he felt had betrayed and abandoned him. Physically, it was far more obvious. Eliezer reeked of a smell comparable only to death. His face was covered with lines of anxiety, his clothes, once well-kempt, were now tattered rags, his body looked malnourished, as it was thin and aged, and his skin resembled a shade of yellow that showed signs of neglect and fatigue. Eliezer looked fully disenchanted and worn from his surroundings. He was fading and shriveling away into nothingness, like a flower slowly shedding away its beauty due to a lack of sunlight. Eliezer pleaded for the boys to stop the senseless abuse, to show mercy. But, on the contrary, like a boar encircled by hunters and hounds alike, Eliezer was thrown to the ground, kicked, and beaten by the boys wearing the tidy gray uniforms. The swastika symbolized a violence and hatred that was unmatched in history. They harassed Eliezer with the relentless-ness and devastation of a hurricane attacking a Pacific coastline.

While the boys maliciously struck, the Angel of War hovered over Eliezer's withering frame, ready to pounce when his body succumbed to death. As the boots landed remorselessly onto his thinning frame, chants from the boys in the gray uniforms sang like a choir, "Down with the Jew! You are the scum of the earth. Down with the Jew! Sellers of your own children! You are our problem. Down with the Jew!" Like a puppeteer manipulating a doll's every move, Adolph looked on in absolute delight at the actions of his underlings. He began to laugh with a hiss that resembled a snake.

IX

Allies Show Resolve

Battle of Midway: Turning Point in the Pacific
A Changing Wind: Russia Turns to the Cold
Italy Surrenders: Crack in the Axis

Time, gliding like a dream, moved on at a rapid pace. As the fight raged on, the years seemed to evaporate like a May snowdrift. Three years had passed since the melee had begun, and an end was nowhere in sight. While Adolph continuously landed blow after blow on Stalin, Winston, in an attempt to keep Stalin in the fight, jabbed the back of Adolph's head.

As Franklin joined in on the action and as Adolph continued his dominance over Winston and Stalin, a cold and stiffening wind began to blow unremittingly through the schoolyard. As if sucked out by a vacuum, the heat dissipated, and the temperature plummeted to subzero conditions. It cut like knives, this air so cold. Like rows of cornfields, the hairs on the backs of the boys' necks stood tall. As an Arctic chill lingered over the schoolyard, it hindered many occupants, no one more obviously than the underdressed and unprepared Adolph. His short-sleeved garments were great for delivering lightning-quick attacks, but they were defenseless against this bitter new enemy, the cold. It would be the cold that beckons Adolph to heed to its might. As a result, his motions began to slow, and his punches began to look more desperate as they attempted to finish off Stalin quickly.

On the other hand, as much as the cold hampered Adolph's actions, it seemed to have the opposite effect on Stalin. As a flower after a drought drinks in the steady, swooping rain, Stalin inhaled the brisk wind to replenish his strength. One could only look on in complete adulation as Stalin raised his broken body from the earth's surface and set his unrecognizable, bloody face inches from Adolph's. Stalin proved to be as unbreakable as a piece of steel. Adolph, who upon delivering his best punches to his adversary's jawline, became deflated as he saw his opponent stand firmly in place. With strength like steel, Stalin's arms quickly encircled and engulfed the deflated Adolph and gave him the squeeze of a Russian bear. As the air slowly drained from Adolph's lungs, he knew that he was in great peril.

Franklin, still standing following Tojo's two surreptitious blows, knew that winning this fight would be an arduous task. There Tojo stood with a look in his eyes that glimmered with inflexible fortitude. In addition, Franklin knew that he could not rest his entire focus on this determined foe, for he knew that Adolph and Benito had to be dealt with as well. He knew that if he was going to join in the struggle with Winston and Stalin, the three boys, who coined themselves the Allies, needed to devise a strategy that would lead to victory over the other three who called themselves the Axis powers — Adolph, Benito, and Tojo.

Tojo was a courageous fighter, who Franklin understood would not surrender without an over-exhaustive effort on his part. Although Franklin was stronger and possessed more resources, Tojo was equally if not more fierce than his much larger adversary. As the two boys squared off, Franklin found himself eating stinging jab after stinging jab from the smaller Tojo. Every time he attempted to deal a shot of his own, Tojo ducked under and stung him like a hornet. However, one punch altered the entire landscape. As if climbing into the mind of Tojo and knowing where he would be, Franklin dealt a punch *midway* up Tojo's torso. The punch landed with such force that it knocked the air out of Tojo and sent him sprawling backward into a defensive posture for the remainder of the fight. He no longer could deliver speedy punches and now would be at the mercy of Franklin's wrath. Like a furious eagle, Franklin swiftly and deliberately clawed his way up Tojo's body until he reached his head.

After a brief meeting between the Allied boys, Franklin, Winston, and Stalin, the Allies planned to expose one crack in the Axis' armor; and that crack was Benito. He did not seem fully committed and repeatedly needed Adolph's aid when he had an altercation with any of the other boys. Hence, the Allies surmised that their first target would be to knock the weaker Benito from the fight. Stalin, who was beginning to turn the tide in his favor with Adolph, would continue to keep his full attention on Adolph, while Winston and Franklin knocked Benito into submission.

After Franklin and Winston hurled an unrelenting combination of kicks and punches toward Benito, like a table bearing too much weight, he collapsed suddenly. Much to Adolph's chagrin, Benito quickly capitulated under the strain and left his two friends to fend for themselves. The first crack in the Axis powers had been exposed and exploited. The momentum by the

Allies created a metaphoric rush of blood that continued to swell for the rest of the fight.

X

V for Victory

D-Day: Beginning of an End
Battle of the Bulge: One Last Flutter
Germany Capitulates: A Country Destroyed
Atomic Destruction

The culmination of the cold weather and the collective might of the Allies began to chip away at the exhausted Adolph. As Stalin's hammer arrived abrasively to the chin of Adolph, it filled Adolph with a crushing sense of defeat. In essence, he was reeling, and things were only about to worsen. To further illustrate, Franklin, while placing Tojo on the ropes, was strong and mighty enough to throw a monstrous blow onto the left side of Adolph's face. The sturdy blow from Franklin dowsed any hope of victory and reiterated the fact that it was only a matter of time before he collapsed in defeat. As a result, while the right side of Adolph's face was being increasingly peppered by Stalin, he now knew he'd continuously catch blows on his left side. In short, Adolph was stuck in between a

rock and a hard place, and his distance between each
of them was rapidly shrinking.

The boys in the gray uniforms continued to kick
Eliezer, and as a result, the glow of life in his eyes became dim. With each boot touching down on the defenseless boy, the Angel of War inched closer and
closer, his metallic cage lowering, readying itself to
place the young boy into its' icy and clammy grip. To
the Angel of War, Eliezer looked cold and faint. He
reasoned that this innocent boy suffered a fate that
would have only been fitting for Lucifer himself.
However, with reluctance, he positioned himself to
set Eliezer into his eternal imprisonment. The cage
door opened, and just before Eliezer heeded to its
grip, the sound of approaching footsteps sent the Angel of War fleeing.

The Allied boys had finally arrived, and they came to
the rescue of the beaten and battered boy. After toss-
ing the gray-uniformed boys off of the ghastly figure,
who lay in a pool of his own blood, the boys in the
gray uniforms vanished as quickly as they had ap-
peared. The Allied boys had to relieve some of the
smaller boys of their gray uniforms, while others
ripped them off quickly in fear of a reprisal for their
crimes. Although forever scarred, Eliezer's life had
been saved by the slimmest of margins.

As the kicks and punches continued to rain in on him from all directions, Adolph moved like a man trapped within a swarm of wasps. Like the smell of a barbecue, defeat hung in the air, and the Allies salivated in delight at the upcoming feast. However, while on the verge of collapse, like a tornado in the middle of the night, Adolph unexpectedly and violently *bulged* forward and crashed into Franklin and Winston with one last valiant attempt. For a brief moment, the punches sent both boys faltering back on their heels. However, as quickly as they rocked back, they recovered and moved forward, their immense weight and might being too much for the weakened and fatigued Adolph. The final pitched effort left Adolph entirely weary and exhausted, and he had nothing left in him. Franklin and Stalin seemed to thrust forward in competition with one another to finish off the dwindling Adolph. Their kicks and punches brought devastation upon him, and he collapsed in defeat.

Stalin, who had not forgotten the earlier betrayal and brutality, when Adolph had stuck him with his knife, viciously beat Adolph with the hammer and sickle until both of his arms became entirely numb. Like a curse from hell, a hate-filled revenge grew out of the soul of Stalin and sprawled upon this now-pathetic figure. Before Adolph could mutter the word surrender, Stalin knelt down, extended his arm outward, and used his sickle to rip the heart from Adolph's chest. The fight with Adolph was finally over.

Upon seeing Stalin finish off Adolph, Franklin set his entire focus on Tojo. One could see that Tojo, while bleeding profusely, should have capitulated long before. However, the honor in fighting to the death eclipsed any notion or inclination toward surrender. With Franklin's own energy to continue the fight in question, Tojo's bravado forced Franklin to unveil something that to that point in history had never been seen before. It was a round and robust object that Franklin lifted high above his head and brought down to a devastating halt on the defenseless Tojo. Similar to a meteor, the object crashed down on Tojo, creating a thunderous sound, and blood exploded from his head like a geyser. Tojo sat dazed and confused— too confused and delirious to really grasp the world around him. While wrapped up in confusion, Tojo failed to utter, "surrender." As a result, with little hesitation, Franklin elevated the object again and slammed it down hard on top of Tojo. Along with the thunderous sound that ensued, a whirlwind of questions concerning morality emerged. However, Tojo, finally grasping the dire pain and destruction the object wrought, surrendered. World War II had come to a close.

Like a farmer who had been plowing all day welcomes sunset, the Angel of War was elated that his work was finally finished. As quickly as it took the shadowy figure to arrive, with as many as 80 million souls left dead in his wake, he departed to find his way back to his comfortable abode... He would rest with a certainty that it would only be a matter of time before these humans summoned his services again. And pain and suffering he promised to bear with him again, if heeded.

The End

Charlie sat on in astonishment. Although the young adolescent did not fully understand the meaning of every transgression, he vowed to find out. "Poppa, that's the greatest story of all time!"

With little warning, Charlie wrapped his arms around Poppa, buried his head into his chest, and gave him a hug of all hugs. "Thank you so much for the best birthday present of all time Poppa."

With a wet mist in his eyes, Poppa uttered, "Thank you Charlie for being you. I am sorry I couldn't figure out a way to wrap your birthday present for you."

Charlie, while wearing a puzzled expression across his face asked, "What do you mean Poppa?"

As Poppa held the book out towards Charlie, handing it over, "Your birthday present from me wasn't to have me read this story to you. It was to give you this book for your tenth birthday."

Charlie didn't have to say a word. His beaming smile said it all.

XI

The Cold War

Germany: A House Divided
The Cold War Begins

As the dust settled over the world following World War II, two large and muscular silhouettes could be seen standing over the horizon. The horizon represented a new day, a new time in history, and a new beginning for the world to adhere to. As the clouds parted, the light shone through, allowing the two silhouettes to become clearer and more visible to an onlooker. Like a heavyweight fighter in the twelfth round, their faces are bruised, blood hemorrhages from fresh wounds, and deep gashes run from the left eye to the chin. One can see the pride glimmering in their eyes ... the pride only a fighter can obtain from overcoming all odds by taking an adversary's best punches, delivering his own decisive and crippling blows that knock an opponent into a dreamy state, and possessing a vision for the future to rest upon the throne of power. As a man beats the dirt off a welcome mat, the two beat the dust from their torn, battered, and beaten clothes. Although bloody and battered, they stand. They stand prouder and stronger than ever before.

Upon further examination, an onlooker can see beaten and incapacitated figures scattered across the barren ground like tomato seeds in a farmer's field. Some of these men rest upon their knees, blood pouring from their open wounds. Others lie face down, using the earth as an uncomfortable respite in hopes of replenishing their strength. As the birds sing songs of sorrow for the eighty million fallen, these men groan in dire pain and plead for help from the two strapping men who eclipse their defeated and weakened states of being.

Although these two men are equally fit in size and strength, they are as alike as a pear is to a cucumber. The man standing on the left preaches to the audience and tries to pitch the fact that he represents freedom, Democracy, and Capitalism. If they want to stand strong and free, they need to allow him to help them attain that. He argues that in his economic system of Capitalism, people will be able to pursue whatever jobs they wish and attain the amount of money that can make them immensely wealthy. The burly figure roars on that if they follow him, the people will be able to control their own destinies, competition will improve the quality of life, freedom of religion will be allowed, and there will be equal opportunity for all.

In an attempt to bellow louder than the other, the robust figure on the right sells the fact that he represents Communism, equality, free health care, and employment for all. He continues to orate to the audience that if they follow him, they will be part of something larger than themselves… part of a community-like state that takes care of all of their needs. He preaches that if followed, there will be no poor who push shopping carts down streets and look all night for shelter from the stiffening cold; that if followed, they will be equipped with the strong leaders that are capable to make the tough decisions in the coming decades.

As the day rolls on, they each attempt to roar louder than the other… truly believing that history would prove them right in the near future. They only stop to gaze upon those bleeding and defeated men lying beneath them… pathetic shells of their former selves. As the groans die down, each and every deflated individual has a decision to make and a question to answer — which man to follow and which man to lean on to help restore them to greatness. All know that whichever one they choose, they will be turning their backs on the other and were to receive no help in the future from the neglected.

No one knew which side would end up standing victorious at the end of the cold and bitter conflict — the Cold War. What they did know was by the end of the century, time would tell which side of history they would stand or fall on. None could predict at that moment, forty-four years later, without a single official shot fired between the two sides, a victor would have his arms raised over an embarrassed and vanquished enemy.

Post-World War II

As the two shadows materialized overhead of the just recently divided German land, one flanking the west, the other the east, each victor had its own ideas of what to do with the devastated nation — the convicted party for two world wars in two decades. The country stretching over the western region of Germany, the United States, hoped to learn from the mistakes brought on by the past. The harsh treatment on Germany imposed by the Treaty of Versailles at the end of World War I and the economic woes associated with it allowed for Adolph Hitler to sell his devilish vision and rise to an unquestioned authority. Upon knowing this, the United States hoped to prevent any future world wars by creating an industrious, economically prosperous Germany. Consequently, the United States argued strongly for Germany to be rebuilt and to become self-sufficient.[xlvi]

On the other hand, the country extending over the eastern region of Germany, with a strong military presence in Germany very prevalent after the war, hoped to keep Germany weak and agricultural-based. One could argue that the Soviet Union was in the right for wanting to diminish the strength of Germany; over the past twenty-five years, Germany was responsible for invading the Soviet Union twice and killing approximately thirty-five million Soviet people.[xlvii] The last thing the Soviets wanted from its despised neighbor, Germany, was to rise again from the ashes and wreak destruction onto its people.

On September 2nd, 1945, with Japan's surrender, the curtain on World War II had finally closed. However, it was on May 8, 1945, that the common enemy of the United States and the Soviet Union no longer bound them together. Germany was defeated, and now there would be growing tensions between the world's only

two superpowers. By late 1944, Germany was a waste-
land. During the war, the constant bombardments,
two invading forces pinching in from the east and
west, and the fact that Hitler refused to surrender toward the end, laid it in complete ruin.[xlviii] There were
twelve-to-fourteen million German refugees who had
nowhere to live and very little to eat.[xlix] Considering it
was thoroughly destroyed, a question needed to be
addressed: what to do with a ruined Germany? The
two options were to rebuild Germany back to its industrial capabilities and potential might or make it an
agriculturally dependent country with little industry.
The answer was that both options manifested themselves into realities. Shortly after the war, Germany
was split into two separate countries, East Germany
and West Germany. The East Germans came under
the authoritative control of the Soviet Union and its
political system, while West Germany's politics were
strongly influenced and shaped by the United States.[l]
Although the people in these two countries spoke the
same language, shared the same history, and bore the
same family trees, the two countries themselves became antonyms to one another. The contrasting and
conflicting economic and political systems instilled in
them created a tense situation that helped to fuel the
Cold War. The division and the actions by the pup-
peteers controlling these two countries, East Germany

and West Germany, put a greater distance of trust between them.

Another question needed addressed: How did the governments and their people in *Europe*, parts of Asia, and surrounding areas get to a point in history where their survival depended upon the monetary and military assistance of one of these two superpowers — the United States or the Soviet Union? European countries, especially in the west, were once such proud nations. It was these western European nations, especially England, France, and Germany, who for centuries, dominated the globe mercilessly… On a scale that would have made Charles Darwin blush in shame. However, much like an Olympic athlete following a horrific accident, they were reduced to a figurative wheelchair. Due to the immense and indiscriminate bombing upon European cities on a magnitude never fathomed before the start of World War II, times were now bleak and urban areas within almost every European country were in need of major repair.[li] Ravaged buildings within these cities had to be rebuilt, brick by brick. The culmination of the bombings during World War II and the food shortages, disease, and economic woes following it knocked many countries on their proverbial knees, leaving them at the complete mercy of these two countries.

XII

Epilogue

"It has been said that something as small as the flutter of a butterfly's wing can ultimately cause a typhoon halfway around the world."
– Chaos Theory

One needs to look no further than the Nile, the Amazon, or the Mississippi River to grasp the concept and underlying meaning of history. Much like a river, history can be impacted by a seemingly miniscule event and trigger a catastrophe. Such changes in magnitude and equivalence to the "insignificant" rain storm in Minnesota that causes the irrevocable floods in Louisiana... all the while, destroying the lives and the homes of thousands. History is full of examples of such lessons. Consequently, one needs to examine history to better grasp the meaning of the world in which he or she lives. Too often in time, people stare at the proverbial rock, without taking the appropriate steps to find what is under it. Furthermore, people view the fall from the cliff as the sole cause of injury, instead of what led one to the cliff in the first place. Generally speaking, we as a human race are either too lazy or too apathetic to discover what is beneath the rock or retrace the steps which led one to the cliff. Instead of falling into complacency, I urge you and interested parties alike to dig deeper and strive for greater understanding.

For example, although historians rightfully note that the Treaty of Versailles was a key antagonist for the start of World War II, American history has oversimplified the conflict into four main topics: an attack on Pearl Harbor, a Holocaust, a mad man, and an atomic bomb. World War II is too broad in scope to be merely categorized into these four topics. In A. C. Grayling's book, *Among the Dead Cities* (in which he uncovers the devastating, yet often neglected Allied bombing campaigns throughout the war, which leveled German cities and civilians alike), he passionately disputes that "history has to be got right before it distorts into legend and diminishes into over-simplification."[lii] Hence, if a person hopes to know the true story of World War II, he or she must research, listen, and interpret the actions of the involved parties.

The characters within this book, some relative nobodies, became magnificent cogs in the machine called history. Through the advantageous prism of hindsight, those relative nobodies were actually much bigger performers than first realized. Upon further inspection of those countries considered minor players during World War II— which are China, Ethiopia, Austria, Czechoslovakia, and Poland— these countries were, in actuality, the sparks that engulfed the forest. They helped provide the stepping-stones which led to the disastrous conflict. History is full of anomalies and events that are seemingly small on scale but in actuality are as in sequential as a number is to an Algebraic equation. Anomalies in history can be found when a relative nobody, if viewed through a prism based off monetary wealth, political influence, or celebrity status, creates the momentum that supplants previous mind-sets, traditions, and ways of life… for better or for worse.

To help reinforce this point of view and to play off the metaphoric correlation between history and a river, Herbert Hoover, the thirty-first American president, rode the Great Mississippi River Flood of 1927 into the Oval Office.[liii] In the hopes of gaining exposure and being viewed as someone who had a willingness to help others in need, Hoover inserted himself in New Orleans at the time of the flood. The combination of media coverage portraying him as a hero, and Hoover rendering himself as one, propelled him up the polls and into the White House. Consequently, had there been no flood, Americans would have been looking for a different scapegoat during the Great Depression… which would probably have been to Hoover's satisfaction.

To further illustrate the cause-and-effect relationship and anomalies in history, look no further than Rosa Parks. When Mrs. Parks stepped onto the bus to go to work on the morning of December 1, 1955, she was as known to the world as a lion is to a penguin. However, her unwillingness to relent in the face of tyranny and injustice as she stepped back onto the bus in the evening, helped fuel a movement that was still in its infancy stage, and crafted her a legacy that has yet been matched by the majority of African- Americans.

Meanwhile, who would have thought the combination of a twenty-dollar bill, a sweater, a president, and two mentally unstable nobodies, could have entirely altered the perception of the American people toward its government? On the twelfth of March, 1963, for just under twenty dollars, a man used the alias of "A. J. Hiddell" to purchase a WWII-era Italian bolt-action rifle. A. J. Hiddell, better known to the world as Lee Harvey Oswald, used the rifle to fire three shots from a sixth-floor window into a motorcade below. Two of those bullets struck and fatally wounded the thirty-fifth US president, John Fitzgerald Kennedy.[liv] A person standing idly by at that point in history would surmise that if life were fair, the proverbial river would stop flowing and allow people to digest the magnitude of what had just transpired. Rather, even with the assassination of a president, it wouldn't be realistic to expect a proverbial river, which is in constant motion, to cease to flow. For this purpose, as Americans attempted to swallow and accept the fact that their beloved US president was a corpse, Oswald, while walking toward a transport vehicle delivering him to a Dallas county jail, was shot and killed by nightclub owner Jack Ruby. A little known fact in history is that Ruby never would have possessed the opportunity to shoot Oswald, had Oswald not asked for a black sweater to be placed atop his T-shirt. The two minutes it took to retrieve the sweater and place it on Oswald was the two-minute window Ruby needed to get into a position to shoot Oswald.[lv] Paradoxically, the reaction caused by the death of Oswald reinforces the chaos theory and the argument that a flutter can cause a typhoon. Although one may feel that Oswald got what he deserved, Ruby's mob and police connections only fueled a plethora (many absurd) of conspiracy theories (some involving the American Government) that manifested themselves into something much larger. Markedly, the killing of Oswald triggered a lack of trust from the American people toward their "deceitful" US government. However, not to get the reader or the author off point, by venturing down the beaten path of conspiracy theories involving the JFK assassination, who would have thought at the time that a miniscule, unknown nightclub owner would help break the lines of trust between America's people and their government?

Although a river can be altered through the creation of a dam, a levy, or a causeway— as it did with Herbert Hoover, Rosa Parks, and Jack Ruby— it also can become a turbulent and determined force that conquers all in its path. As a result, history provides a plethora of examples in which people have been swallowed up in the proverbial river's wake. To further illustrate, there have been individuals who have had all of the chips resting under their noses, all of the determination to climb Mount Everest, and all of the odds in their favor to beat Vegas' best casinos, but yet, mysteriously enough, they came up short. Some would call it fate, others would call it bad luck, or one would call it a force of momentum that was bigger than any single person's actions… whether for good or for evil. History is full of times when nature beckons destruction, and man must heed to its might. Vladimir Lenin, Chiang Kai-shek, and Colonel Claus von Stauffenberg are all exemplary individuals who help to reinforce this argument.

To start, Lenin, the leader of Russia and the Bolshevik Party, concluded that Joseph Dzhugashvili, better known to the world as Stalin (meaning "man of steel" in Russian), had to be removed from any political relevancy within Russia. Stalin, in Lenin's mind, was a mentally disturbed personality who would be extremely dangerous if head of the Soviet state.[lvi] Additionally, Lenin believed that Leon Trotsky would be the better fit to fill the role that Stalin had ambitions to attain. Consequently, in April of 1923, Lenin planned to use the party congress to remove Stalin from any relevancy. However, mysteriously enough, Lenin suffered a series of strokes a month before, that ended his tight political grip over Russia and halted the momentum needed to topple Stalin from power. Rather than Stalin disappearing from the annals of history, this momentous force allowed Stalin to jockey and position himself to violently remove Trotsky and other political opponents who stood in his path. Unfortunately for countless Russians, Stalin ruled the Soviet Union from 1924 to 1953, with an unquestioned, totalitarian rule. It was a totalitarian and ruthless rule that included two purges and the death of twenty-plus million Russians. Just think, had there been no stroke, there would have more than likely been no Stalin.

Chiang Kai-shek, who ruled China under a nationalist rule between 1930 and 1949, provides another remarkable example of someone swept up by this momentous current. In China, from the 1920's through 1949, a bitter civil war ensued between the nationalist and Communist forces. Through the advantages of research and hindsight, it was the Long March between 1934 and 1935 that played the decisive role in the conflict. Unbeknownst at the time, it was this year that led to a Communist China fifteen years later (through the present day), and beginning the merciless rule of Mao Zedong. By the same token, this turn toward Communism meant that China would become a dangerous enemy of the United States for most of the Cold War. It was during the Long March that Chiang and his nationalist forces had forcefully placed Mao and the Communists on the figurative ropes and on the literal run. The Communist forces of fifty thousand had been ruinously crushed and stood at the mercy of Chiang's five hundred thousand men. Unfortunately, it will be mercy that Mao receives. Incredulously, instead of finishing the Communist forces off, Chiang, due to a variety of extenuating circumstances, lets Mao's small force flee to northern China and stand under the protection and safe haven of its northern, Communist Russian neighbor. The first of these extenuating circumstances was Chiang's own miscalculation of how disastrous it would become in allowing the Communist forces to regroup. Secondly, Chiang's nationalists were the ones primarily fighting the expansionist-minded Japanese forces, who had occupied Manchuria in 1931. Subsequently, Chiang desperately sought Russia's military supplies and intelligence support to combat Japan. Hence, Chiang did not want to jeopardize the backing from Moscow, by crushing its Communist ally in China. Lastly, there was the fact that Russia held Chiang's only son hostage, to be played as a bargaining chip for Chiang, in case of an instance such as this. As a result, the story unfolded with Mao replenishing his weapons and soldiers and creating the time and momentum needed to propel him to power and force Chiang to flee to Taiwan in 1949.[lvii] Unfortunately for millions of Chinese, Mao immensely admired Stalin's approach to Communism and his callous management traits. As a result, through acts of murder, war, starvation, and disease, it left up to sixty-million of Mao's own Chinese people dead.[lviii]

Lastly, the date was July 20, 1944 and there lay a briefcase concealing a bomb, only feet away from Adolph Hitler. Colonel Claus von Stauffenberg, in a conspiracy that would implicate Irwin Rommel, carried out a plan to assassinate Hitler (code-named Valkyrie). Following a complete collapse of the German army on the eastern front against Russia and the successful D-day invasion on the western front, the war against the Allies had now become hopeless. As a result, Stauffenberg and a relatively small number of German leaders attempted to take control of the military and its government. This would have enabled Germany to sue for peace and spare countless lives. However, history had something else in mind. On a last-minute whim by Hitler, he changed the location of the meeting from a concrete-laden bunker to a wooden barracks.[lix] As a result, the air pressure from the explosion penetrated through the thin wooden walls, and the attempt to kill Hitler in an East Prussian headquarters failed. The blast from the bomb left Hitler with only superficial injuries, and the rest, as they say, is history… Germany fought on, and as a result, thousands of more men, women, and children died, and millions of "dissidents" continued to meet the dead man's fate.

Considering *Kids Will be Kids* is a fictional piece based off of non-fictional events, I am quite certain that critics could refute some of the arguments made within this book. However, it is difficult to fill the proverbial shoes of an entire country with the small feet of a child. In addition, World War II is far too complex to decipher fully with a short story. Hence, if anyone is offended or was disappointed by this book, I would like to reinforce that that was not my intention in any way. To the contrary, I hope that you enjoyed this book and that it conveys a fresh and profound insight on the history of World War II.

In regards to the topic, I chose to write about World War II because I have always been fascinated with the event. World War II incites so many people to study it because it offers unlimited interests to a variety of different readers. This fact is a consistent reason why the majority of my students state their favorite event to study in history is World War II. As mentioned earlier, the war contains countless stories of murderers, heroes, horrors, battles, weaponry, tactics, blunders, bravery, deception, persecution, courage, romance, preparation, science, leadership traits, sociology, etc. Arguably, no other historical event offers an equal amount of experiences and documented tragedies. An estimated 60 to 80 million people perished during that horrendous war... a number that no human being can fathom. What people can fathom, are the applicable lessons it offers each of us… if we are willing to open our minds to them.

Sources

I again would like to thank every author below for taking the time to write some very impressive work. Over the years, I have been able to pull something profound out of each of these works and apply them within my classroom. The works below and countless others have instilled in me the confidence and ability to present history in a more story-telling manner. Without these authors, I would not have found the energy, the passion, or the know-how to travel down the path to become an author. James Bradley and Bill O'Reilly's penmanship are brilliant and ingenious, as both truly bring history alive and write with such a fresh approach. John Mosier's work in *The Myth of the Great War*, truly gave me the ability to teach World War I in an enlightening and profound manner and I was able to apply some his research to this book. The two films I used from A&E were also such fine and captivating pieces of art. I highly recommend both and my students within the classroom are enthralled when I show each of them. So again, in short, I want to thank the fine work from these authors, producers, and directors below. They are samples of work that will continue to prove the test of time.

Suggested Reads:

Suggestions on books that you should read covering WWII:

End of War- David L. Robbins
This is one of my personal and underrated favorites on the topic of World War II. This is a fictional piece, based off of non-fictional events. David Robbins does a terrific job of intertwining an American journalist, a Russian infantryman, a Berlin woman, and each of the major Allied leaders during World War II. Mr. Robbins does an outstanding job of showing each of their individual successes and failures throughout the war and using the war as a major backdrop. This is really worth reading and he deserves more credit for this immensely underrated piece of literature.

Flyboys- James Bradley
James Bradley is one of the great historians and authors of our day. *Flyboys*, a national bestseller, is nothing short of brilliant. Although this is non-fiction, he does a great job of bringing the Pacific campaign to life, shedding light on the horrific crimes committed by the Japanese soldiers during the war, and scratching beneath the surface in the Pacific theater.

Imperial Cruise- James Bradley
James Bradley does it again in *Imperial Cruise*. This book serves as a prequel to *Flyboys*, and shows how Japan in the mid-1800's, in its hopes to compete with Imperial western powers of the time, changed from an agrarian culture to an industrial and militarized one, leading it on a collision course with the United States at Pearl Harbor.

The Cold War: History in Hour- Rupert Colley
Rupert Colley provides some fresh perspectives and insights
into the start of the Cold War. He does not neglect World
War II, instead he uses it as the catalyst to the beginnings of
the nuclear age and the Cold War. Again, if you want to get
the biggest bang for your buck on the complex and lengthy
Cold War, this is a great book to either start or end with. You
will be floored with how well Mr. Colley is able to maximize
your time and understanding of the content.

The Duel: Eighty-Day Struggle Between Churchill & Hitler- John
Lukacs
John Lukacs does a wonderful job of climbing into the minds
of two of the most sought after leaders of the 20th century,
Churchill and Hitler. He offers many fascinating and less
known morsels in his book: from Hitler's thoughts on America, to Churchill and Hitler's style of military engagement, to
who Gandhi supported in the war. Overall, this will give you
a better perspective of how and why Churchill and Hitler
operated the way they did during World War II.

WW2: A Short History- Norman Stone
As you can see, Norman Stone's work was used over and
over again within this book. He offered up some amazing
World War II information in his *World War II: A Short History*
that I had never stumbled across before in other books. Although I have read multiple books covering World War II,
and have been drawn to each of them, I may have leaned on
this one the most in this book. Mr. Stone did a fantastic job
of following Mr. Colley's blueprint on a less is more ap-

proach, and this is definitely worth the read. He magnificently covers and intertwines many events from before, during, and after the war.

WWII: History in Hour- Rupert Colley

Rupert Colley captures major events in history and follows a less is more approach in his writing. By less, I don't mean in terms of scope or learning, however in regards to less time and more precision for the reader. I believe that Mr. Colley has hit a home run with his *History in an Hour* series and will continue to impress and educate readers for a long time.

[i] Harris, Alex & Brett. *Do Hard Things: Teenage Rebellion Against Low Expectation*. Multnomah Books, 2001.

[ii] Bradley, James. *Flyboys: A true story of courage*. 1st ed. Boston: Pg. 29. Little, Brown & Co., 2003. Print.

[iii] Mosier, John. *The Myth of the Great War: A New Military History of World War I*. 1st ed. New York: Harper Perennial , 2001. Print.

[iv] Mosier, John. *The Myth of the Great War: A New Military History of World War I*. 1st ed. New York: Harper Perennial , 2001. Print.

[v] Rittenmeyer, Nicole, prod. "The Third Reich." Prod. Seth Skundrick. *The Third Reich*. A&E Television Networks: 2010. DVD.

[vi] http://www.ushmm.org/wlc/en/article.php?ModuleId=10007428

[vii] Chang, Jung. *Mao: The Unknown Story*. 1st ed. New York: Anchor Books, 2005. Print.

[viii] Stone , Norman. *World War II: A Short History*. 1st ed. New York: Basic Books, 2010. Print.

[ix] Stone , Norman. *World War II: A Short History*. 1st ed. New York: Basic Books, 2010. Print.

[x] Stone , Norman. *World War II: A Short History*. 1st ed. New York: Basic Books, 2010. Print.

[xi] Rittenmeyer, Nicole, prod. "The Third Reich." Prod. Seth Skundrick. *The Third Reich*. A&E Television Networks: 2010. DVD.

[xii] Rittenmeyer, Nicole, prod. "The Third Reich." Prod. Seth Skundrick. *The Third Reich*. A&E Television Networks: 2010. DVD.

[xiii] Rittenmeyer, Nicole, prod. "The Third Reich." Prod. Seth Skundrick. *The Third Reich*. A&E Television Networks: 2010. DVD.

[xiv] Bradley, James. *Flyboys: A true story of courage*. 1st ed. Boston: Little, Brown & Co., 2003. Print.

[xv] Bradley, James. *Flyboys: A true story of courage*. 1st ed. Boston: Little, Brown & Co., 2003. Print.

[xvi] Stone , Norman. *World War II: A Short History*. 1st ed. New York: Basic Books, 2010. Print.

[xvii] Stone , Norman. *World War II: A Short History*. 1st ed. New York: Basic Books, 2010. Print.

[xviii] Stone , Norman. *World War II: A Short History*. 1st ed. New York: Basic Books, 2010. Print.

[xix] Bradley, James. *Flyboys: A true story of courage*. 1st ed. Boston: Little, Brown & Co., 2003. Print.

[xx] Stone , Norman. *World War II: A Short History*. 1st ed. New York: Basic Books, 2010. Print.

[xxi] Stone , Norman. *World War II: A Short History*. 1st ed. New York: Basic Books, 2010. Print.

[xxii] Lukacs, John. *The Duel: The Eighty-Day Struggle Between Churchill and Hitler*. 1st ed. New Haven: Yale University Press, 2001. Print.

[xxiii] Colley, Rupert. *World War Two: History in an Hour*. 1st ed. London: Harper Press, 2011. Print.

[xxiv] Colley, Rupert. *World War Two: History in an Hour*. 1st ed. London: Harper Press, 2011. Print.

[xxv] Taylor, Alan. "World War II: Operation Barbarossa." *In Focus*. 24 07 2011: n. page. Print.

[xxvi] Stone , Norman. *World War II: A Short History*. 1st ed. New York: Basic Books, 2010. Print.

[xxvii] Colley, Rupert. *World War Two: History in an Hour*. 1st ed. London: Harper Press, 2011. Print.

[xxviii] Bradley, James. *Flyboys: A true story of courage*. 1st ed. Boston: Little, Brown & Co., 2003. Print.

[xxix] Stone , Norman. *World War II: A Short History*. 1st ed. New York: Basic Books, 2010. Print.

[xxx] Lukacs, John. *The Duel: The Eighty-Day Struggle Between Churchill and Hitler*. 1st ed. New Haven: Yale University Press, 2001. Print.

[xxxi] George, Simon. "WWII From Space." A&E Home Video. May 2013.

[xxxii] Stone , Norman. *World War II: A Short History*. 1st ed. New York: Basic Books, 2010. Print.

[xxxiii] Colley, Rupert. *World War Two: History in an Hour*. 1st ed. London: Harper Press, 2011. Print.

[xxxiv] Atkinson, Rick. *The Day of Battle: The War in Sicily and Italy.* 1st ed. New York: Henry Holt and Company, 2002.

[xxxv] Padrusch, David. "Art of War: Suz Tzu's Legendary Victory Manuel Comes to Life." A&E Home Video: 2009.

[xxxvi] Gisevius, Hans. *Valkyrie*. 1st ed. Cambridge: Da Capo Press, 2009. Print.

[xxxvii] Rittenmeyer, Nicole, prod. "The Third Reich." Prod. Seth Skundrick. *The Third Reich*. A&E Television Networks: 2010. DVD.

[xxxviii] Bradley, James. *Flyboys: A true story of courage*. 1st ed. Boston: Little, Brown & Co., 2003. Print.

[xxxix] Colley, Rupert. *The Cold War: History in an Hour*. 1st ed. London: Harper Press, 2011. Print.

[xl] Colley, Rupert. *The Cold War: History in an Hour*. 1st ed. London: Harper Press, 2011. Print.

[xli]http://admin.bhbl.neric.org/~mmosall/ushistory/mapsgraphs/WWI%20WWII%20Compare.jpg

[xlii]http://admin.bhbl.neric.org/~mmosall/ushistory/mapsgraphs/Rise%20and%20Fall%20Axis.jpg

[xliii] Mosier, John. *The Myth of the Great War: A New Military History of World War I* . 1st ed. New York: Harper Perennial , 2001. Print.

[xliv] The Churchill Centre & Museum at the Churchill War Rooms, London. http://www.winstonchurchill.org/learn/speeches/speeches-of-winston-churchill/128-we-shall-fight-on-the-beaches.

[xlv] Manchester, William. *The Last Lion: Winston Spencer Churchill Defender of the Realm, 1940-1965.* New York: Little, Brown and Company, 2012.

[xlvi] Colley, Rupert. *The Cold War: History in an Hour.* 1st ed. London: Harper Press, 2011. Print.

[xlvii] Colley, Rupert. *The Cold War: History in an Hour.* 1st ed. London: Harper Press, 2011. Print.

[xlviii] A. C. Grayling, *Among the Dead Cities* (New York, Walker Publishing Company, 2006).

[xlix] Rittenmeyer, Nicole, prod. "The Third Reich." Prod. Seth Skundrick. *The Third Reich.* A&E Television Networks: 2010. DVD.

[l] Colley, Rupert. *The Cold War: History in an Hour.* 1st ed. London: Harper Press, 2011. Print.

[li] A. C. Grayling, *Among the Dead Cities* (New York, Walker Publishing Company, 2006), 2.

[lii] A. C. Grayling, *Among the Dead Cities* (New York, Walker Publishing Company, 2006), 2.

[liii] John M. Barry, *Rising Tide: The Great Mississippi Flood of 1927* (New York, Simon & Schuster, 1998), Audiobook.

[liv] O'Reilly, Bill. *Killing Kennedy: The End of Camelot.* 1st ed. New York: Henry Holt and Company, 2012. Print.

[lv] King, Stephen. *11/22/63.* 1st ed. New York: Scribner, 2011. Print.

[lvi] Lechnitz, Diane, dir. "Hitler and Stalin: Roots of Evil." Writ. Anthony Potter. A&E Television Networks: 2010. DVD.

[lvii] Chang, Jung. *Mao: The Unknown Story.* 1st ed. Pg. 128-135. New York: Anchor Books, 2005. Print.

[lviii] Chang, Jung. *Mao: The Unknown Story.* 1st ed. Pg. 128-135. New York: Anchor Books, 2005. Print.

[lix] Gisevius, Hans. *Valkyrie.* 1st ed. Cambridge: Da Capo Press, 2009. Print.

18783093R00074

Made in the USA
San Bernardino, CA
28 January 2015